The
Holy
Spirit

The Holy Spirit

BY NORMAN PITTENGER

A PILGRIM PRESS BOOK
from United Church Press Philadelphia

Library of Congress Cataloging in Publication Data

Pittenger, William Norman, 1905-
  The Holy Spirit.

  "A Pilgrim Press book."
  1. Holy Spirit.
BT121.2.P57   231'.3   74-10839
ISBN 0-8298-0284-3

United Church Press, 1505 Race Street
Philadelphia, Pennsylvania 19102

Contents

About the Author

Norman Pittenger is senior resident, King's College, Cambridge, England, and member of the faculty of divinity, University of Cambridge. For thirty years he taught at the General Theological Seminary, New York City. Dr. Pittenger is widely known in Europe and the United States for his travels and lectures and is the author of some sixty published books, including such popular ones as *Making Sexuality Human, Love and Control in Sexuality*, and *Trying to Be a Christian*.

Preface

This study of the doctrine of the Holy Spirit is one result of my retirement from academic work. After some thirty years of teaching at the General Theological Seminary in New York and another five years of work in supervising research students in theology at the University of Cambridge, I am now free to spend most of my time reading and writing as I wish and when I wish, delivered from the responsibilities of regular lecturing, conducting seminars, and guiding students in their theological studies. One of the things that has engaged my attention in this leisure is a consideration of the work of the Holy Spirit—a subject which earlier I had not given the attention which it deserved, although in several books and in a few essays I had touched upon it.

Two things have become clear to me. The first is that the doctrine of the Holy Spirit has always been rather like a "poor relation." Little has been written about it, save in passing, while a kind of polite nod has been given to it in teaching and in preaching save on the Feast of Pentecost when *something* had to be said. This neglect is being remedied in our own time. There have been several excellent books on the subject, among them those of Hendrikus Berkhof, *The Doctrine of the Holy Spirit* (1964); George S. Hendry, *The Holy Spirit in Christian Theology* (1956); H. Wheeler Robinson's earlier *The Christian Experience of the Holy Spirit* (first edition 1928 and a subsequent edition in 1947); and that exciting and prophetic work by C. F. Raven, *Creator Spirit* (1927). More recently we have had J. V. Taylor's *Go-Between God* (SCM, 1973). In most of these, save Raven's and Taylor's books, the concern has been specifically "religious," in that the work of the Spirit has been seen primarily if not exclusively in the response made by people, either personally or in the church, to the revelation of God in Christ.

This brings me to the second matter that has become clear to me as I have pondered the subject. The *cosmic* significance of the Holy Spirit, in *all* history and in *all* nature, has been strangely neglected. In a lecture which I gave in New York as far back as 1957 (published along with other lectures by various theologians in a volume called *Preaching the Christian Year*), I stressed the wider cosmic and historical work of the Spirit, attempting to relate this to the personal and ecclesiastical work of the same Spirit. A reviewer criticized me vigorously for venturing to go, as he said, beyond the limits of biblical thought in this stress. Evidently he did not recall a considerable number of Old Testament and apocryphal passages to which I had alluded, nor did he see the implication of some things said about the Holy Spirit both in the Johannine and Pauline literature. Yet the fact that he could write in this way indicates something of the attitude I have in mind. The Holy Spirit is most certainly often mentioned as present in men's response to God's self-revelation; he is seen in the "sanctification" of believers; and he is regarded as at work in the Christian church—but outside those circles, in the secular areas of experience and in the vast world itself, he has not often been looked for nor has he been understood as at work.

This book is intended to be a "persuasive," as older writers used to say, against these two tendencies. It is not my only purpose, but also one of my major concerns, to urge that the Holy Spirit is a *very* important subject to which we should give full attention. At the same time I urge that any rounded and inclusive view of God and the world must take account of the operation of the Spirit throughout the universe, in the natural order, and in the historical realm, as well as in the personal and social religious experience of men in the Christian fellowship of faith.

I am keenly conscious of the imperfection of what I have written as well as of the brevity and inadequacy of treatment. I can only plead that like all theologians I am a finite creature who can do no more than the best of which he is capable; while for the brevity of this book I can apologize by saying that I am convinced that at the moment what is needed is not so much the big compendious volume as the shorter suggestive writing. The time is not yet with us for the production of full-scale theological books; there is too much reconstruction going on, too many doctrines to be reconceived, too much material at hand for this task, for anybody to presume to present a new "system" of Christian thought. That day will come, I am sure, but it will be delayed for many years. In any event, I know very well that I am not the person to attempt it. So I send forth this book in the hope that it may give hints and offer suggestions which others will find useful. That is all; but at my age and in this time, perhaps it is enough.

Norman Pittenger

1

The Importance
of the Problem

As if it were yesterday, I remember some remarks made by my old teacher in theology, Marshall Bowyer Stewart, professor at the General Theological Seminary in New York City. Dr. Stewart was discussing the doctrine of the Holy Spirit in traditional theology. "You might almost say," he remarked, "that the Holy Spirit has been 'the forgotten man' in Christian thought." Then he went on to point out how after the period of christological controversy and settlement in the early church, ending with the Chalcedonian Definition of A.D. 451, the question of the Holy Spirit was raised through the appearance of such heresies as Macedonianism. "And you could almost say about *that*," he commented, "that the Holy Spirit said to theologians, 'What about me?'" But as he noted not very much was done, save to insist on the full deity of the Spirit as against a sort of "Arianizing" of his relationship to the Godhead.

He said something else, equally important. "People often ask why we don't have a *cult* of the Holy Spirit—worship directed towards him. Maybe it is better *not* to have such a cult; maybe it is better to remember that we don't so much pray *to* the Spirit as pray *in* him." And he illustrated this by pointing out that very

11

few traditional collects are addressed to the "third hypostasis" of the Godhead, while only a few devotions such as *Veni Creator* are directed to him.

This book might be described as a commentary on Dr. Stewart's remarks. It is indeed true that the Holy Spirit has not been written about to a great extent although in recent years Wheeler Robinson, some continental divines, one or two American writers, and in Anglican circles, Bishop Cockin, Bishop Fison, Canons Raven and J. V. Taylor have published books on the subject. One of the purposes of this book is to say something theological about the Spirit. But another purpose is to show why Dr. Stewart's concluding comments are also sound and right— why the Holy Spirit is not properly the object of a special variety of Christian devotion, and precisely for Dr. Stewart's suggested reason: We are to pray *in* rather than *to* the Spirit.

In this book we shall have something to say about the scriptural material which bears on the Spirit. We shall also discuss the work of the Spirit in the community (the "secular" community and the Christian fellowship) and in human personality, but we shall also look at the work of the Spirit in the natural order—an aspect of the situation very often overlooked or forgotten in Christian theology. Yet we shall not approach this doctrine of the Holy Spirit, nor shall we develop a possible way of interpreting the "third hypostasis," in what might be styled a conventional manner. For the background of and the context for our discussion will be the conceptuality which nowadays goes by the name of "process thought." That is to say, we shall look at the work of the Holy Spirit, and from that work consider the "person" of the Spirit in the light of a dynamic, processive, societal understanding of the world and man and God. The philosophical orientation will be taken from the extensive writings of thinkers like Alfred North Whitehead and Charles Hartshorne, to which frequent reference will be made.

At the same time, however, we shall argue that a serious reckoning with the material found in holy scripture is in a general sense accordant with the dynamic, processive, and societal way of seeing the world and man and God—and hence, of seeing the Holy Spirit in his operation in the world and in his relationship to the total "reality" of Godhead. This will mean that we

12

shall not look at the Bible as if it were a mine from which theological nuggets may be extracted, one after another, and then arranged in some appropriate pattern. That is not the right way to use the Bible, however popular and conventional the method may have been in much Christian theological work. What will interest us is *what the Bible is saying*, in, through, and by the words which are used in saying it. What does the scriptural witness indicate? What were the intuitions or insights of the biblical writers as they responded to, and sought to make sense of, their experience as men who felt themselves in some profound relationship with a divine reality greater and more compelling than any merely human or natural fact?

I should not for a moment presume to claim that this book will be exhaustive or conclusive. It is my hope that it will be suggestive, proposing lines of exploration and ways of thought that may be helpful in considering the meaning of the Holy Spirit in religious, and specifically in Christian, experience. For I am convinced that the matter is important and that it is for want of due attention to the Spirit that much else in Christian theology has gone astray. Two obvious examples of this are in the treatment of the nature of the Christian church and in the discussions of ministry and sacraments. Precisely because the Spirit has been forgotten, these matters tend to be regarded mechanically. It is the Spirit who *gives life* to them and *only* the Spirit.

In Christian hymnody one of the most frequently used phrases describes the Holy Spirit as "the Spirit of Love." Nor is this merely because love rhymes with above, a word which the hymn's author wishes somehow to introduce into his verse. The Spirit is described in this fashion because in Christian experience, as well as in the New Testament witness as a whole (particularly in the Johannine literature and the Pauline epistles), love is indeed the chief "gift of the Spirit." This obvious fact introduces us at once to a consideration which will be central in our study. Whitehead and others have commented on the strange neglect of love as the chief criterion in Christian thinking about God. They have noted that power or "being" or will has been given preeminence, whereas the "Galilean vision," in Whitehead's phrase, would require that persuasion, goodwill, or love-in-action should be put first in all our thinking about God—and about everything else, for that matter.

But if love is thus central, and if we attend to this reiterated use of words about love in connection with the Holy Spirit, any adequate treatment of the Spirit must be in terms of that love. If God *is* personalized and personalizing Love-in-action, as the New Testament evidence should make us boldly affirm, then whatever we say about the Holy Spirit must be profoundly in accord with that view. In what sense, in what way, *is* the Spirit "the Spirit of Love"? And the use of the uppercase L here is of first importance, for the Love about which we are speaking is not merely human love, significant as that is and invaluable as a clue to the very nature of the divine reality himself. The Love which is here in question is *cosmic* Love—it is God himself. Hence it is Love, God as Love and Love (in its supreme sense) as God, with whom we must concern ourselves.

One result of such serious attention to Love will be that whatever is said about the Holy Spirit will relate him to the activity in which love-in-the-world is awakened, developed, increased, and shared. We must not anticipate what will be said in our further discussion. Yet we ought to see that ideas of the Spirit as exercising a coercive control of creatures in whom he is at work cannot be consonant with the key concept of God as Love—a concept which is no mere invention of men's minds and no interesting philosophical suggestion, but rather the consequence of the meeting of men with someone who both cares for them and concerns himself with them in their actual concrete human situations. And this is done focally and decisively, as Christians believe, in the Man Christ Jesus in whom God, Love-in-action, was so vividly "en-manned" that newness of life was engendered in those who responded to him.

I have just now mentioned church, ministry, and sacraments as three areas of theological discussion—and, one might add, involving practical Christian behavior—where failure to recognize the reality and the role of the Holy Spirit has had damaging effects. There are others, of course. Indeed, almost every aspect of the traditional theological scheme requires the life-giving Spirit to perserve it from deadness, dullness, and absurdity. But perhaps because of the ecumenical concern which has been so significant in recent years, the three areas that I have mentioned are of particular importance. Each of them has been bedevilled by a tendency to a mechanical, legalistic, static interpretation of the sort that makes it impossible to see the "graces" given in and through means, agencies, and rites which do not conform to certain prescribed patterns. I venture to say this so strongly since I myself, in early books and essays in which I dealt with the church, was guilty of precisely this error, although on my own behalf I must add that I always sought to interpret the church itself in organic and vitalistic terms. Yet even in doing so, I failed to take account of the freedom, spontaneity, freshness, and unpredictability which a proper emphasis on the Spirit would have enabled me to stress when I sought to present the Christian church in dynamic and vitalistic terms.

Now that I have come to see this, I can agree with criticisms made of those early writings, more particularly of my Bohlen lectures *His Body the Church* given in the early 1940's, by Stephen Neill and Dr. F. W. Dillistone, who pointed out that even the relatively liberal ecclesiological doctrine which I urged lacked the openness which emphasis on the Spirit would have given it. It was, as Bishop Neill remarked, ultimately a matter of "one's doctrine of God." And my doctrine of God, while entirely orthodox by most standards, was deeply in need of three things: first, a suitable stress on the Spirit's work in the Christian fellowship and in individual Christians; second, a fuller awareness of the total biblical picture, in which the Spirit is so strongly present; and third, a view of the divine reality which refuses to accept the more static, absolutist terms of the classical theology and instead lays its emphasis on the dynamic, processive, and societal side—such as I have mentioned earlier in this chapter and which I myself learned in the period immediately after those lectures when I came to read, ponder, and then accept the validity of the writings of Whitehead and Hartshorne.

But to return briefly to church, ministry, and sacraments. The church is "the Body of Christ." That is not only a Pauline concept, but is also suggested in other ways by other images—e.g., the vine-and-the-branches in the Johannine writings. But how are we to understand this? Despite the obviously organic connotation of the phrase, most Catholic thinking until recently has

15

substituted an *organizational* picture for an organic one. The hierarchical principle, both in Anglican and Roman Catholic circles, has been interpreted in unchanging terms; in fact, the church looks more like a machine than a body. The faith itself is stated in propositional idiom which succeeds in identifying the words used in defining it with the thing defined—e.g., to question the Chalcedonian definition is equivalent to questioning the reality which that definition was concerned with stating. The stress on tactual succession by the laying-on-of-hands of a bishop, himself in the "correct" line of descent from some supposed dominical or at the latest very primitive period of Christian history, has led to a denial of the "validity"—although nobody could bring himself to deny the "efficacy" in some limited sense—of the sacramental ministrations of those who through no fault of their own, perhaps, have never received ordination to a Catholic priesthood. When one contrasts this with the New Testament portrayal of the first Christian community, in all its variety and spontaneity, one may well wonder at the way in which the human desire for order, regulation, and control has destroyed, to all intents and purposes, the "glorious liberty of the children of God."

To say this is not to reject the need for continuity of life in the Christian church; it *is* to call in question the strong tendency to confine the working of God to channels which happen to approve themselves to certain types of theological tradition. Happily, in both Anglican and Roman Catholic circles today, the emergence of a "new look," itself (dare we say?) the work of the Holy Spirit in spite of "the traditions of men," has led to very considerable modification of this organizational conception of the church, sacraments, and ministry. Yet, as recent attempts at securing church union have demonstrated, there are sufficient numbers of ecclesiastical leaders who either frankly maintain the other view or have a secret hankering after it. In another book,* I have tried to discuss this problem, largely in terms of that status-seeking which so often dominates the clerical mind. And I do not mean status in the sense of social position, but status in the sense of a secured ecclesiastical privilege which

* *The Christian Church as Social Process* (Philadelphia: Westminster Press, 1971).

16

sharply distinguishes, to the degree of separating, the clergy from the "people of God."

The same is true with respect to the sacraments. Not only have dogmatic definitions often been regarded as almost more important than the concrete meeting with Jesus Christ which the eucharist enables, but also the whole way of insisting on the proper formulae for consecration of the elements; the necessity for a specific kind of ministerial ordination to "validate" the sacraments; and the occasional dismissal (which I have often heard) of "non-Catholic sacraments"—that is, those whose minister is *not* in the "right" succession—as nothing more than ordinary "eating of bread and drinking of wine," with no essential communication of the living Christ; have shown all too clearly a mechanistic and legalistic understanding of the matter. Likewise the confusion of mind which identifies the Western isolation of confirmation from baptism with the reality of things, despite the verbal acknowledgment that the Eastern church sees things differently, has led to an attitude toward admission to the eucharist that cannot be defended in the light of historical evidence and that in any event confines the working of God to those particular channels which appear satisfactory to traditional theology.

At all these points, I should urge that an adequate recognition of the work of the Holy Spirit would save us from absurdity and blasphemy. What is more, a recognition that the Holy Spirit himself is by no means confined to the Christian church but "blows where he lists" would have averted the danger of making the Spirit adjectival to the church. In patristic thought the Word of God, the "second hypostasis" of the Blessed Trinity, is not confined to the specific incarnation in Jesus of Nazareth but is seen operative throughout the cosmos, in all human history, and in every person. So also the Holy Spirit is not confined to the ecclesiastical community but is operative in the cosmos, in human history, and in every person—above all, in all response to whatever is known of God as he seeks unfailingly to disclose and give himself to his human children. The mechanical view of church, ministry, and sacraments is bad enough; equally bad, if not worse, is the notion that the Holy Spirit himself is the possession of the church in its narrowest interpretation. Even so broad-minded a theologian as Charles Gore was inclined to talk in these terms. I also recall the struggle which some of us were obliged to make to secure that in a quasi-official statement of the "teaching of the church" room was made for the nonecclesiastical activity of the Spirit in the world —this despite the fact that the Old Testament is full of that conviction of the widest possible range of the Spirit's work.

I have written the above paragraphs with no intention of indulging in polemic, although their controversial character will be apparent. Nor in this book do I purpose to spend time in such discussion. My aim is to suggest a positive and intelligible conception of the Holy Spirit and his work, in the light of the biblical witness and in the context of a dynamic and societal view of God, with its consequences in a similarly dynamic and societal view of the world and of persons. I am convinced that only in this way can we be delivered from parochialism and from that legalist and mechanistic conception to which I have referred.

The context of the Spirit in the dynamic and societal view just mentioned should be given due emphasis. In the following chapter this will be developed at some length, although in other books I have argued for the adoption of this conceptuality as generally necessary if we are to do a useful job in reworking Christian theology today. This is for two reasons. The first is that most informed persons today accept just such a position, however inadequately they may be able to articulate it; the only possible metaphysical stance at this time follows such lines. The second reason is that such a view is much more in accordance with the biblical perspective than a more static and absolutist position. Once we get back to the teaching of scripture, with its mythological picture of the cosmos, of God, and the relationship between the two, what we find portrayed is a living and active God at work in a world for which he cares and with which he identifies himself in loving concern, while that world itself is open and plastic, with enormous variety and with the appearance within it of genuinely new things. A metaphysic which talks in terms of things, entities, substances, and the like, that are either inert and static or lacking drive and movement, has never adequately served Christian theology, although many theologians have found themselves attracted to it or inescapably forced to use it for their purposes. A processive conception is much more attractive, although it requires of us that we give up our human demand for absolutes of the totally unchanging sort and for the kind of perfection which allows no room for development and growth.

In working out a viable conception of the Holy Spirit we require something else too. We must be keenly conscious of the meaning of human existence, with its depths and heights, its unseen as well as overt motivations, and its continuing relationship with and dependence upon environmental factors for its true development. We must see people themselves, as well as the communities to which they belong, as "becoming" rather than as merely "being" something. There is a forward thrust in human existence of which we must take account. At the same time there is a belonging, a togetherness with other people that is indelibly human, so much so that no single individual can be said to "exist" apart from one's relationships, however subtle and invisible these may appear, with others of the human race. A "rugged individual," to the degree that such a one is isolated and separated from other people, is a truncated and perhaps even an *inhuman* creature. The relevance of these two facts to the work of the Holy Spirit will be argued in the sequel.

Furthermore, we must note that in this human existence, as well as in the world where such existence is enjoyed, there are hidden depths. These have been called by some "sub-personal," but that is a mistake. They are rather to be seen as the profoundly visceral, emotive, affective—in one sense of the term, "aesthetic" or marked by a "feeling-tone"—qualities which characterize all existence. A Western rationalistic reading of experience has so strongly stressed the explicitly conscious and intellectually apprehended aspects of things as they are, that it has neglected to a startling degree these deeper but equally real elements in the world. Many years ago Prof. Filmer Northrop of Yale University wrote about the need for Western man to take into his thinking what he styled "the aesthetic component" so much part of Eastern or Oriental thought. I am sure that Professor Northrop's point was well taken. People *live* at many levels or in many dimensions; they are influenced and affected in many different ways. Intellectuals are often prone to forget this. Perhaps one of the consequences of the overintellectual emphasis in Western philosophy has been a theological rationalism which fails to give due attention to the way in which personal existence and group existence are both genuinely lived and experienced in ways that include conscious awareness, to be sure, but are by no means exhausted in that awareness. Persons *feel*, in the most profound sense we can give to that word.

As a result of the overintellectualizing of theology there has been the danger of assuming that realities are only as real as our conscious thought about them. Thus there are some theologies which seem to take it for granted that God, for example, is a reality only to the degree that his human children attend to him, think about him, and believe him to be *there*. If people *say* that they have no rationally experienced sense of God's presence or activity, then it is thought that God cannot be at work in their life. But surely response to the divine initiative is possible at most diverse levels and through most various dimensions of existence. It is not necessary that we be vividly *aware* of what is going on. The peril in such theologizing as I have just criticized is that we shall confuse our concepts with the whatever-it-is that those concepts are intended to point toward and so far as possible identify. There is a kind of abstracting of concrete realities which produces an identification of such abstractions—words like God or salvation or life-in-Christ, etc., not to mention incarnation and atonement—with the relationships and the depths of experienced reality to denote which the abstractions have been devised. What matters, we ought to see, is not the abstractions themselves but that which they serve to convey; and it may very well be the case that these realities and relationships are deeply known and enjoyed by those to whom the abstractions, as they stand, make very little sense.

This is no plea for irrationalism. It is a demand that our rational exercises, with the intellectualizing that follows from them, shall be seen in their context and with the most profound regard for the richness both of human experience and of the world-setting for that experience. I think that the truth is that persons live much more deeply and with much wider ranges of experience than *any* words can contain or express. At best, the words are useful counters; we should use them carefully, criticize them, and employ whatever logic may be appropriate in respect to them, but we should never assume that they are exhaustive of the fullness of the experience to which they point and from which they took their meaning.

At the beginning of this chapter I quoted some remarks from my old teacher in theology. I conclude with a consideration of another comment of his, which seems to me equally apt and important. Professor Stewart said that "in one sense, perhaps, we can call the Holy Spirit the most anonymous 'person' in the Godhead." This, he urged, was not only because the Holy Spirit's function, so to say, was to provide the "atmosphere *in* which we pray—or, if you like, let him pray *through* us." It was also because the Holy Spirit appears to be concerned largely with pointing toward the everlasting Father as that Father is disclosed to us in the incarnate Son; and because the working of the Holy Spirit in us is not toward making any claims for his own visibility and obviousness but rather is toward making our own response to God the more real and vitalizing.

These remarks tie in well with what I have been arguing concerning the nonconceptualized depths of human experience, as well as of the world at large. I shall urge that the best way to understand the function of the Holy Spirit in the context of the triunitarian picture of God is as the *response* of "deep to deep." But that response, in order to be real and true, need not always be consciously apprehended and described for what it is. To require this would be to succumb to the fallacy of assuming once again that our human understanding, or even worse our human descriptive capacity, exhausted the reality of God's working. Very often, perhaps most frequently, the working of God is *not* thus consciously apprehended and hence not rationally described. The task of theology is to attempt to clarify what is known in Christian and other human experience, in the light of the act of God in Jesus Christ; it is not to provide a straitjacket in which God must be confined, lest in his operation in the world he get "out of our control."

What is more, the working of the Spirit, like all the activity of God, is greater than the specific operation which occurs in the "religious realm." The *world* is the Lord's; the Spirit is

21

active in *every* nook and cranny of the creation. Much that he does has nothing to do with religion in the narrower definition of that word. I was once criticized for saying that when D. H. Lawrence spoke of his poems as written, not by himself, but "by the wind that blows through me," he was really speaking of the "anonymous" act of the Holy Spirit as he inspires people with poetic insight into the way things go in the world. It was pointed out that the scriptures do not talk of the Holy Spirit in that way but have only to do with his activity in conforming people to God or to God in Christ. But did not my critic have altogether too restricted an idea of God and of God's ways of "coming to men"? Taking the example I have cited, may it not be the case that in the poetic insight there is in fact a response to some working of God which is not specifically *religious* but nonetheless is wonderfully divine?

Baron Friedrich von Hügel was warned by the Abbé Huvelin, his spiritual director, to avoid anything that would "narrow or canalize" the Christian faith. That warning has an even wider reference. We must avoid any sort of theological statement which suggests a narrowing of God or a "canalizing" of his self-disclosure and self-expression to the ecclesiastical, the scriptural, or the specifically "religious" (in the usual sense of that word). If we do not earnestly seek to avoid that mistake, we are very likely to fall into the dreadful position of blasphemously rejecting many of the places, the areas, and the persons where God may most certainly be revealed and active—and revealed precisely because he is active.

When Frederick Denison Maurice said that we tend to give people "religion" when what they are thirsting for is "the living God," he spoke the truth. It is equally, perhaps more importantly, true that we must be alert to the living God wherever he is found—which often enough will not be in "religious" channels at all and most surely will not always be in those particular spots where we can say "God," as if the vocable were easily and simply applied to some places and not to others. If God is greater than our hearts, as the apostle said, he is also greater than our minds.

It is for this reason that I shall have much to say about the more pervasive or universal operation of the Holy Spirit, rather

22

than limiting myself to talking about the church or even about religion as such. Nor do I consider this an "unorthodox" way of discussing the subject. For in the grand central historical Christian tradition, there has been a much more open and generous spirit in this respect, as in the matter of the Logos or Word or "second hypostasis" of the Godhead, than many seem to know. "The Holy Spirit filleth the world and all things have knowledge of the Voice": That sentence from the Jewish tradition has been taken into Christian liturgical rites for the observance of the "Feast of the Spirit," Whitsun or Pentecost. I take it to be the charter for the sort of universalizing of the meaning of the Holy Spirit to which I shall give considerable attention in this book.

2
A Dynamic View of the World

There was a time when both ordinary people and learned scholars thought that this world in which we live was once for all created at some time in the past—perhaps a few thousand years before the beginning of the Christian era, perhaps longer ago than that, but none the less a finished product of which sense was now to be made. Theologically this conception meant that God had decided to "make a world," having previously "existed" in absolute reality as a self-contained and unrelated being. Whatever "relationships" there were had been entirely internal to him; for did not the doctrine of the Holy Trinity speak of Father, Son, and Holy Spirit as "persons" indwelling one another? This mutual indwelling or circumincession (*perichoresis* in Greek theology) provided for God a sufficient "object" of love: The Father loved the Son, the Son the Father, while the Holy Spirit was the bond of love between them—a bond which in some mysterious sense was also "personal." But apart from this internal relationship, God *as God* (that is, God in his fullness as Father, Son, and Spirit) had no necessary relationship, not even a willed relationship, with anything external to him "before the creation."

However, by an act of will God in his goodness—a goodness which desired some expression, not by imposition upon himself but by his own nature—created a finite universe. Everything in it was made by him to be as perfect as finitude would permit; but once made, there it was. Even if some great Christian thinkers, Augustine for one and Origen for another, had a less static view; even if Thomas Aquinas now and again wrote as if the change from potentiality to actuality required what nowadays we should call a "process"; and even if to some there was an educative movement through revelation, as to Irenaeus in one way and the Cappadocian fathers in another—granted all these, the *picture* of the world, as the simple man understood it and as the learned man took it to be, was static. In a word, evolutionary thinking in the sense in which we all know it today, whoever we are, had not yet become general and, indeed, had not yet been more than glimpsed by the very occasional genius.

It was in such a world that Christian theology in its traditional form was worked out; the "system" of Christian theology, whether in its Catholic or its Protestant viewpoint, presupposed a world that was once-for-all made. Hence it could do no other than state the Christian faith and its implications in such terms. Christian theologians of the past are not to be blamed for this; they were not omniscient, and there is no reason to accuse them of willful obscurantism. There are few things more silly than to indulge in criticism of this type. Nor do we in our own time have any reason to suppose that to us all the truth has become plain. One day, doubtless, our descendants will regard us as out-of-date and wonder why we thought and wrote as we did. This should not prevent our doing the best we can with what we do know, but it should make it impossible for us to sneer at our ancestors who did the same.

If it is improper to blame theologians of the past for working out their doctrinal statements in terms of the best knowledge they had, it is equally wrong for us to remain content with the form of statement which they produced. We know perfectly well that the world is not a static order; we know that it was not created, more or less as it is, some thousands or millions of years ago. A theological construction which presupposes these ideas cannot make any sense in an entirely altered world-view. One

25

of the many reasons for the failure of Christian teaching to win the assent of thoughtful people today is just here in the insistence, by a not inconsiderable number of spokesmen for the Christian faith, on the retention without change of those older formulae. Or, if some sort of change is seen to be necessary, the sort which is advocated is simply "translation" in the common meaning of that word: putting an old idea without any modification into another language. But such a translation makes no more sense than the simple retention of the formula in its unchanged language. The fact is that any translation which is other than literal is bound to reckon very seriously with the way the context in which an idea is stated radically alters the content of the idea. In an entirely different picture of the world, many traditional notions simply will not fit; they are like flies in amber, preserved for centuries but dead. Or they are meaningless surds, which have no proper place in the equation and are only retained because they have some aura of sanctity about them.

This is not the place to develop at length the point we have just made. It must suffice to say that concepts of God that fitted well enough into a view of the world which was static and which had some meaning when the creation was thought to be a "finished product," are impossible when we accept a view of the world which is evolutionary and which knows there are no such "absolutes." This does not imply that *no* concept of God, with *no* continuity with past concepts, can be entertained; it has been the mistake, I think, of the "death of God" school to make this assumption. On the other hand, very serious, even startlingly radical, modifications are required in how we think about the supremely worshipful and altogether excellent whom we name God. Something of what is here intended will appear in the sequel. But we must now consider in more detail what was indicated in the title of this chapter: "a dynamic view of the world."

The publication of Charles Darwin's *Origin of Species* in 1859 was the event which first brought vividly before the educated reading public the notion of a world in evolutionary movement. Darwin's work had been preceded and was accompanied by other scientific study which ran along similar lines; his own immediate concern, as the title of his epoch-making book indicates, was with the rather limited question of the way in which the various species of living creatures came to their present form. His conclusion, based on extensive observation and brilliant theorizing, was that the development occurred through "natural selection," in which "the fittest" survived. But Darwin's view, originally of interest only in the field of biology, was capable of extension—and during the second half of the nineteenth century, this extension was made. Perhaps Herbert Spencer's many volumes were as influential as anything else, but Thomas Henry Huxley (who popularized "Darwinianism") and others also played their part.

The result was a view of the world which emphasized change, but the change was regarded by many as nothing more than the rearrangement of particles of matter, infinitesimally small, into more complicated patterns—from "homogeneity" to "heterogeneity," as Spencer put it. The cosmos was seen more on the analogy of a great machine than anything else; here the continuing influence of the stress in Newtonian and post-Newtonian science on physics, and hence on a mechanistic picture of the creation, was very strong. Change there was, to be sure, but it did not include the appearance of genuine novelty in the world. The biologists may have been uncomfortable about this, since after all they dealt with *living* entities, not "dead matter"; yet it was possible for a biologist to be a mechanist, especially when the alternative was an incredible "vitalism" predicating some strange entelechy or ghost-like spiritual essence distinct from, and incapable of study along with, the physical body or the cellular structure.

But in the latter years of the nineteenth century and the first decade of the twentieth, the fascinatingly written philosophical works of the French biologist-turned-philosopher Henri Bergson, opened the door to "creative evolution," a term which was also the title of Bergson's most famous book. Here the stress was on novelty. The world was not a machine; it only appeared so when we took a momentary cross-sectional picture of it. In Bergson's own illustration, it was like a motion picture film. The film itself shows a flowing series of events, and that is the way the world really is. But it is possible to stop the film at a certain point, and then one has a "still" in which there is no flow or movement—that is the way the world appears to the mechanistically minded scientist. But that is *not* the real world; it is an artificial abstraction from the world.

An old friend of mine who grew up in the latter half of the nineteenth century and was in his thirties when Bergson's book was published, has told me of the enormous sense of liberation which a reading of Bergson brought him. The world had seemed to him to be a "block universe," in William James's famous phrase; *now* there was a sense of openness and of freedom, because novelty was as much a reality in that world as it was felt by him to be in his own experience as a living man. Doubtless my friend was typical of many, since Bergson's views found a large following.

Of course, it is not my intention to commend the Bergsonian theory as it stood, and, indeed, Bergson himself somewhat modified that theory in his later writing. The notion of an élan vital or vital thrust throughout the world, as the basic reality of things, may have been too picturesque a way of putting the story. The point is that during the period of, say, 1859 to 1910, something very important happened to the way in which people looked at nature and at themselves. The dating is rough enough, to be sure; the *fact* is perfectly clear. Before, there had been general acceptance of a static picture of the world, created at one fell swoop. Afterward, any reflective person, and eventually any educated person, had to recognize that the world was an evolving one, in which there was change and movement. At first this had been seen in mechanical terms, but soon it had to be interpreted in *dynamic* terms.

Philosophical thought, as is always the case with new scientific discovery, was at first slow to accept the implications. But before long books began to appear on such topics as "emergent evolution" (the title of a famous set of Gifford lectures by Dr. C. Lloyd-Morgan), and a philosophy of evolution made its appearance. Such a conceptuality was basic to Spencer's writings, as we have noted. These appeared in the nineteenth century itself, but the view gained ground on every side. Perhaps a phrase from the Scots philosopher A. S. Pringle-Pattison sums up with admirable brevity the position which from the early years of this century has been accepted as true: "continuity of process with the appearance of genuine novelty."

The use of the word process in that quotation from Pringle-Pattison is significant. For following the publication of enormously detailed books by such thinkers as Samuel Alexander, Lloyd-Morgan, General Jan Smuts, J. E. Boodin, and many others, the Gifford lectures of Alfred North Whitehead were published under the title *Process and Reality* (1929). That title indicates the contention of the lectures—*reality is a process*. We are in a world which is not made up of "things" moving in space and through time; we are in a world in which the "actual entities" are occasions or events or occurrences. In other books Whitehead developed his theory in many directions. But his "vision," as he called it, was constant: It was the vision of a dynamic world, characterized by what he styled "creative advance," and interpenetrative and interrelated so every event must be seen as involving a "prehension" (a grasping or being grasped, with varying degrees of intensity) by other events. Here is a picture of the whole cosmos as "social process"—movement toward particular goals which each occasion aims at actualizing out of the vast range of possibility, movement in which no given moment can be isolated from past events or apparently contemporary or future ones, movement in which new occasions make their appearance. And in order to account both for the orderliness of the advance and for the emergence of the new, Whitehead found it necessary to speak of *God*. But his concept of God was not the accepted notion of an utterly transcendent "unmoved mover," "first cause" or "absolute reality." Rather, it was a concept in which God is both chief causative agent in providing initial aims to each occasion *and* final "affect" in receiving and using, for his own and for the creation's enrichment, the achievements wrought out as the several occasions (by their own decision) select among relevant possibilities those which tend to the actualization which is their "subjective aim." Hence God is immanent, indeed "incarnate," in the world-process; his transcendence is his inexhaustibility of resource, his indefatigability in luring the occasions to fulfillment, and his faithfulness to his overarching purpose. This purpose is a sharing of good, known in the free decisions of the occasions; it is

29

the realization of love. For to Whitehead the "persuasive" aspect in the world-order, with its lure, was more basic than the sheerly coercive element. So he worked out a view where the Johannine text, "God is love," might be taken as the key or clue to the whole enterprise. Nor did Whitehead overlook or minimize the patent presence of evil in the process. But for him evil was to be interpreted as the "drag," the "backwater," the deviant routing, the imperfect or fallacious decision of the occasion as to its own true fulfillment or satisfaction. This, rather than something radical in the creation (as though an enemy power had entered in, or through some aboriginal or historical "fall" the very creation itself had become a corrupted mass), constituted evil.

It is interesting that during the years when such a vision was being elaborated the distinguished French paleontologist Pierre Teilhard de Chardin was thinking along the same lines. His philosophical-theological writings on the subject could not be published during his lifetime, since the authorities of the Roman Catholic Church and of his own Society of Jesus refused to give the necessary permission; his essays were circulated only in duplicated form among friends. After his death, however, these writings were published; one of them in particular has been so widely read that it is now one of the most celebrated books of our time: *The Phenomenon of Man.* As Dr. Ian Barbour has demonstrated in several recent essays, Teilhard and Whitehead were saying much the same thing, though they were unknown to each other. There is evidence that somewhere along the way, Teilhard had read a book or two by Whitehead, but he does not mention this in his own essays. Whitehead seems to have known nothing of Teilhard's work.

What is significant for us is that through the wide dissemination of Teilhardian views in recent years and through the work of "process philosophers," as well as the availability of scientific knowledge through wireless, television, paperbacks, etc., the informed public takes for granted a dynamic, processive, or evolutionary interpretation of the world. Nor is this only among the educated classes. For the media of communication, like television and wireless, as well as the public press and the very large sale of popular expositions for ordinary readers, have instructed literate people of all types. One could almost say that

today nobody with the slightest pretension to intelligent awareness looks upon the world as static and "fixed," or thinks of creation as accomplished at some one moment in the past.

What I now want to do is to see how the dynamic view of the
world is relevant to our conception of God, and hence to our
understanding of what is meant when Christians speak of the
Holy Spirit. Hence the remainder of this chapter will be
devoted to a spelling-out of the dynamic view with special reference to the divine activity in the world to which (or to whom)
we may give the hallowed name God.

The first thing to say is that such a process conception or
dynamic view of the world has a real place for God. Indeed, that
is a far too simplistic statement. A dynamic view of the world
requires a concept of God; that concept is integral to the "vision
of reality" which it offers. This is not only because thinkers who
accept this position feel bound to do justice to the unquestion-
able fact that "religious experience" is a reality, although they
would indeed wish to stress this. Far too many people, of all
ages and cultures, of all classes and types, report some sense of
"meeting" with a suprahuman realm, some awareness of a
"more" which both succors them in their need and demands
from them a response in commitment and responsibility, for the
"religious experience" to be dismissed as an aberration of men-
tally disordered or emotionally disturbed men and women.
Furthermore, the great religions have claimed the loyal allegiance of too many intelligent and reflective people to make it
possible to call everything that they have to tell us an illusion.
But the basic reason for the emphasis on the reality of God by
process thinkers is that the dynamic character of the world with
its structured pattern requires what God alone can supply: an
explanation of or accounting for how things happen the way
they do, with the ordering they show and the drive they
manifest.

It is a major axiom of process thought that what we find it
necessary to say about God cannot be in complete contradiction
to that which it is necessary to say about the world. Whitehead
stated this axiom in a sentence that has often been quoted and
frequently misunderstood: God, he said, is not to be regarded
as "an exception to all metaphysical principles, invoked to save

31

their collapse," but is "their chief exemplification."* Many who quote those words think that what is there asserted is a reduction of God to *merely another instance* in the world-process, or perhaps to that process itself when seen in a certain light. Whitehead intended, however, as the context plainly shows, that any view of the totality of creation (and with it, of God) must be capable of statement in a form which will be reasonable and coherent throughout. Furthermore, he is telling us that the way things go in the world is indicative of the nature of God and his activity, or else there is an intolerable dualism set up between explanation and that which is being explained. The use of the adjective all is important too; Whitehead himself allows for certain exceptions, such as God's persisting through "the perishing" of the world's "occasions." The main point to stress, however, is the relationship which process thinking finds between the dynamism of the world and the dynamism of God, between the social interrelationships of the world and the way in which God himself is at work in the world, and between the experience of movement toward a goal known to us and its analogue in the divine purpose. God, whose functions we shall discuss in a moment, is himself a "living" God—thoroughly dynamic and not a static "thing" nor a "substance" understood in such static terms. He is related to the creation in a give-and-take fashion, able to receive from it as well as ready to give to it. There is an analogy here between God and the sociality both of human beings and of all occurrences or events, however apparently simple these may seem. Finally, the human awareness of aim toward the fulfillment of which decisions are made among the possibilities relevant at every successive moment has its analogy in God with *his* aim—an aim which will both fulfill him, as our aim fulfills us, and provide him with opportunity for enhancement of his activity in the creation.

But what does God *do*? What "function" does he serve?

In the first place, God knows, in his wisdom, the whole content of the possible; as Peter Hamilton has phrased it, he envisages the "whole continuum of possibility." But he does more than envisage or know this. He provides, from that realm, the

* Alfred North Whitehead, *Process and Reality* (New York: Macmillan, 1967), p. 521.

"initial aim" or intentional purpose for every creaturely occasion. These aims must come from somewhere; if there were no giving of such initial aims, each with its distinctive quality, there could be no novelty, for the world would then be a *stasis,* a settled affair, not a realm open to new emergences. Once the aim has been given, the creaturely occasion is free within limits to make its own decisions among further possibilities presented to it. But only *within limits.* For God functions as what Whitehead styles "the ultimate irrationality," which is a perhaps not fortunate way of saying that there must be some limits beyond which the creative advance cannot go if it is to be creative advance. More briefly, God not only provides "initial aims"; he also sees to it that these aims, like everything else in the process, are so ordered that harmony, not chaos, may be achieved. It is here, especially in levels lower than those where free decision (such as we know ourselves to make) can be made in real awareness of the implications, that God must employ a minimum of coercion—but only a minimum and only for an end that will guarantee good.

God also functions as the "lure" which stimulates and attracts each occasion to move toward its fulfillment. When the event sees, with however small or great conscious perception, its own aim—its "subjective aim" in Whitehead's words—it is drawn to reach that goal, to "become itself," to realize in subjective fullness what initially was its intention. But it needs to be invited to this movement; it needs to feel the "lure" of its own satisfaction. In working in this way, God molds and shapes the impingement upon each occasion of influences from other occasions. There may be an element of chance or risk here for which Whitehead might have made greater allowance; but at the same time there is a working in and through the process so that prehensions (a word whose explanation will be given shortly) are available which will be for the best realization of goals.

Finally, God also receives into himself, in what Whitehead and others have happily named his "consequent nature," all the good which is accomplished in the creation through the decisions made by the many occasions for their own proper actualization of possibility. As each event affects every other event, so each event also affects God. Whatever is good, he receives and enjoys and uses for further good. Whatever is not susceptible of such use—that is, whatever is characterized by "drag," "backwater," deviation of aim, rejection of possible fulfilling—God "prehends negatively." That is to say, he extracts from it such good as it may contain but the rest is "lost" precisely because it is a negation of creative goodness rather than a step toward it.

We have previously spoken of "prehension." As good a translation of this term as one can offer would be "grasping"— not merely intellectual *com*prehension, not only imaginative *ap*prehension, but also that deep feeling of influence which profoundly affects and modifies the recipient. The world is a world of *mutual* prehensions because it is a *social* process, in which every occasion is most intimately related to all other occasions. This relationship may sometimes appear slight; it may gradually fade away almost to nothingness. Yet it is always there. It is an insight which the poets have phrased for us. Tennyson in "Flower in the Crannied Wall" spoke of how the knowledge of one thing, a flower, would open up to us a sense of everything, provided that we *really* knew that flower. Francis Thompson said much the same in his poem about Christ on the Thames: If we but turn a stone, we "touch a wing." Dante wrote in the *Divine Comedy* of the "in-folding of all things"—and added the specifically theistic note that this is "in God." Here too most process thinkers would agree.

For in general the concept of God which dominates this conceptuality is of a pan-*en*-theistic sort. This is not a very familiar term to many of us; it is to be distinguished sharply from *pantheism*, in which God and world or God and nature are identical. Pan-*en*-theism means "everything *in* God"; it might just as well be reversed to say, "God *in* everything." Which of the two one chooses will be determined, very largely, by the matter under consideration. All is *in* God, in that in his inclusive awareness, his wisdom, his purpose, and his love, everything is contained, whether actual facts as actual or possibilities as only possible. God is *in* all, in that his activity is omnipresent throughout the creation. All is present to him and all is the recipient of his loving care. As an American adolescent, using

34

schoolboy slang, put it, "You can't play 'hooky' from God." You cannot run away or escape from him.

Yet when we say this, we should not imply that God is always consciously known to his creatures. The probability is that most of the time, it is through his "secular functions," to use another Whiteheadian phrase, that God is seen active in the world. Only by "attending" to him, which is what prayer is classically defined as meaning, can we be aware of him in a vivid and conscious fashion. Nor should we desire to penetrate the secular veils or incognitos which God wears so much if not most of the time; very often it is better to reverence and respect the functioning which we can observe, without at every moment trying to name it for what ultimately it is, the working of God. The reason for this ought to be clear. If we disregard the secular channels and the areas that do not clearly demand the use of the divine name, we are very likely to engage in a "confusion of categories." That is, we will be tempted to introduce the wrong explanatory and descriptive concepts into our thinking, and the result will be muddle-headedness. One instance of this is the unfortunate habit of people who think themselves very religious and who insist on dragging the word God into a discussion of such matters as social justice. The area under consideration requires use of economic, legal, political categories; it is not the place where the word God functions as a term to which immediate and easy reference may be made. Yet social justice attained by economic, legal, and political action (and whatever other means are necessary) is not only the will of God secularly manifested; it is attained through his luring men to think and act in a responsible way—although doubtless most of the time this ultimate interpretation does not occur to those most active in such matters.

Now what does all this come down to, so far as the Holy Spirit is concerned? The plain conclusion is that any doctrine of the Holy Spirit must be a dynamic one, in which the "operation of the Holy Ghost" (as the liturgical phrase has it) is seen as supremely dynamic. Indeed, the Holy Spirit has generally been conceived in such a manner—one might say that he is the one "person" of the Godhead to whom, in classical theology, dynamism is always attributed. So far, so good. But we need to press this point and press it very hard. First, what is true of

35

him is true of God as such. That ought to be an elementary theological truth. If it is not, the basic Christian doctrine of God has been forgotten. And second, the activity of the Holy Spirit should be seen in every range and reach of the creation. This has not always nor even often been appreciated; hence the "churchifying" of the Spirit by more "Catholic" Christians and the "individualizing" of the Spirit's action in personal religious life by more "Protestant" Christians. I believe an awareness of the cosmic dimensions of the Spirit's working is absolutely essential to any sound doctrine of him, and I think that the dynamic view of the world enables us to see more readily how this cosmic dimension can be asserted and its truth maintained.

In later chapters we shall have much to say about the work of the Holy Spirit in the world, in the Christian fellowship, in people's lives, in worship and in prayer. But before we take up these matters, we must examine the background in scripture and Christian theology for statements about the Spirit. Further, we must also attempt some formal definition of *who he is*—he who in the Nicene-Constantinopolitan creed (so familiar to us from its frequent repetition in the eucharistic liturgy) is called "the Lord, the Giver of life."

3

Biblical Thought and Theological Development

The biblical material relating to the Spirit is most diverse and even contradictory. Sometimes the Spirit is represented as "the breath of God" which gently works in the world, as in the creation narrative in Genesis where the "Spirit moved on the face of the deep." Sometimes the Spirit comes as a mighty force which overwhelms the person or persons to whom he comes. Again he appears as an ecstatic power which produces wild speech and wilder actions. Further the Spirit is the "voice of God" which speaks to the prophet or seer and communicates to him the divine will, purpose, or warning.

With such a variety of senses in which the Spirit is mentioned in the Old Testament, it is indeed difficult, although not impossible, to construct a coherent picture of him. Since our purpose is not to provide a sketch of biblical theology, we need not concern ourselves with the details of the many different ways in which, in the Old Testament especially, Jewish thought made its attempt to work out some concept of the Spirit of God at work in the world. Three observations will suffice.

In the first place, it is apparent that the experience of the Spirit is related to a general background in which spirits were

37

regarded as present in and active throughout the life of nature and of men. In the religious culture in which Judaism had its origin, there were good and evil spirits near at hand and liable at any moment to work for the good or for the woe of men. The spirit might seize someone and unpredictably force him to act in a strange manner. It might dwell in some mysterious place such as a rock or a tree. The spirit also might be in a storm or some other natural occurrence. Whatever else these spirits were, they were vital and dynamic; and one of the necessities for primitive peoples was to find some way of dealing with them. Sometimes this was done through diviners or other supposed specialists, to whom recourse was had by the ordinary member of the tribe or community. Such men were experts in the handling of the spirits.

The background of Jewish religion is the culture of the fertile crescent in the Near East. To forget this is to commit the historical absurdity of supposing that Judaism developed with no roots in the past and no influence from the environment. To remember it is to see that what did happen in the development of Jewish thought was a purification, a moralizing, and a rationalizing of beliefs and practices that were general through that part of the world where the ancient Hebrews had their home.

One of the contributions of the great prophets, beginning with the earliest like Elijah and Elisha, and even before them with Samuel, was to "moralize" and "order" this experience of spirits at work in the world and in people's lives. The spirits were related to the high God of the Jewish people, Jahweh; they were no longer regarded as apart from his controlling power. At the same time, there were the evil spirits; these presented a problem. They could be regarded as "false spirits" or "lying spirits." But whence did they come and how were they related to the supreme God Jahweh who had revealed himself as the God of power and with whom alone the Jews felt they had to do? At the very first, and for some time afterward, it could be thought rather naively that Jahweh sent or gave or used spirits, both good and bad. They constituted, so to say, his court or entourage, and they were Jahweh's means of communicating with his people for good or for ill. Yet as the process of development went on, Jahweh was more and more understood to be a

38

power for goodness, rather than sheer power. Thus it was next to impossible to think that the experiences of destructive and harmful spirits could be seen as part of his working.

As time went on and still other influences were brought to bear on the thought-patterns of the Jews, the evil spirits were taken to be manifestations of a demonic or destructive agency in the world who eventually came to be called Satan. Originally Satan did not have any such role. He was the "testing spirit" sent by God to try people's souls and to prove whether they were good or bad (so in the book of Job—and doubtless, long before the writing of that story, in the earlier thinking of the Hebrews). Now, perhaps due to the subtle effect of Iranian or other religious ideas, Satan was the "chief" or "prince" of all evil spirits in the world; as such he was the "adversary" who sought to undo the good which Jahweh through his own good spirits was accomplishing in the world.

But the evil spirits were a very present factor in the experience of the people; "the air was full of them," we might say. Jahweh was concerned with battling them and overcoming them. So, in the times just before and contemporary with the life of Jesus, the demonic powers were the enemy to be fought, both by Jahweh and by his people. To "cast out demons" was to do God's will in the world. On the other hand, the good spirits were God's messengers. Sometimes they were his angels, acting for him in the affairs of men. Sometimes they were none other than God himself at work in the creation; and it is this last view which became the right one in the eyes of the greatest Jewish thinkers. God sent his *own* spirit; he came in spirit to the people whom he chose. The spirit of God strengthened those to whom God sent him; the spirit gave them insight into God's purpose and will; he worked through all good things, initially making them share in God's plan and then using them to accomplish that plan.

In the second place, while the spirit of God was now seen primarily at work in human lives, the same spirit was also found in the course of nature. Exactly how this wider view came to develop is by no means clear. But certainly by the time of the writers of the Wisdom Literature, a few centuries before the Christian era and then on into the last century B.C. and the first century A.D., it was possible to speak of "the spirit of God" which "filled the world," which was an agency to carry out the divine purpose, and which "sweetly ordereth all things." The cosmic functions of the spirit of God were not formulated in any clear way, but they were recognized as real and highly important. Often there was imprecision in the use of terms. The "wisdom of God," "the word of God," the "power of God" were names which could be given to the activity of God in his creation; but so also could "the spirit of God." In general, perhaps, we can say that the immanent operations of God could all be styled, without too much precision of terminology, the work of the spirit of God, the wisdom of God, or the word of God. The one distinction which seems to have been made, more or less consistently although by no means with great care, was between God's working *on and with* his world or *on and with* his people, on the one hand, and a more internal activity, felt *within* the created "spirit of man" and specially shown in the intensity of response made to the former activity. That is to say, despite the confused use of language and the impossibility of making a neat distribution of terms, the two types of experience were seen as related but distinct: God as operative *alongside of and upon* nature, history, and human lives and God as operative *within and through* these.

In the third place, the spirit of God was known both in personal experience and in social experience. While the spirit was likely to come uninvited and unexpected to a particular man or woman, he was in a very special sense also the spirit known in the life of the "chosen people" as a whole. This conception was also inchoate and unformulated, but it was the hope of the prophets that one day the spirit would be visibly manifest in the whole life of Israel. Moses' desire that "all the Lord's people" should be "prophets"—that is, possessed by the spirit—led to Joel's expectation that some day the same spirit would be "poured out on all flesh"—on all Jews, as the "chosen" of God, and perhaps also on people of every race and faith.

The event of Jesus Christ made a difference in many ways. Every belief and practice found in the Jewish community had to be reconsidered in the light of that event, more specifically, in the light of the extraordinary experience of "new life" which the disciples and their followers had known as they responded to Jesus. This Christian experience was indeed an experience of God, but it was an experience mediated through the event of Jesus. And here we are talking not only of his teaching and his "mighty deeds" in the days of his flesh, but also of the resurrection appearances through which he was believed to have continued his presence among them and in terms of which he was taken to be the decisive act of God. God must be interpreted in terms of the coming of Jesus and his risen life, and anything that was said about God must be seen as illuminated and modified or corrected by what had now occurred.

Jesus had overcome or defeated the evil powers in the world; that is what the Cross had placarded before men. But Jesus was also the medium through whom the spirit was now seen as given to the world. Hence the spirit of God was also the spirit of Christ. Paul seems to have used both terms with practically the same meaning. He was not working out a careful theology; he was writing about his own "new life" and using whatever terms were at hand to convey what that life signified and what it could mean for those who shared in it. Furthermore, the criterion by which it was possible to determine whether or not the experience of "spirit" was indeed a meeting with God himself was now whether or not the experience was in accordance with what was declared about God in Jesus Christ. Here the Johannine insistence on "testing the spirits, whether they be of God," is of great importance. Here too Paul's establishment of the true nature of the "gift of the Spirit" through a descriptive series of its character as "love, peace, long-suffering," etc., has its place.

The Spirit of God which is the spirit given through life with and "in" Christ is now interpreted as a working of God through people which will conform them to the pattern of moral and spiritual excellence which Jesus Christ revealed. Thus we can identify the Spirit of God and of Christ when we see "upbuilding" in the life "in grace"—that is, in the favor of God and in the strengthening which that favor imparts to persons. But this was not so much an individual matter as a sharing in the "fellowship of the Holy Spirit," the Christian community of faith and worship and obedience that Paul called "the Body of Christ" in the world. The Spirit was the Spirit known in the

41

church, although not exclusively and only there. The late Prof. Joseph Haroutunian, in his admirable article in *Dictionary of Christian Theology*,* has rightly stressed this community aspect of the Spirit as understood in the primitive Christian church whose thinking is reported and reflected in the New Testament. It is too bad that he could find space to allude only in passing to what he correctly notes was also in that thinking, namely "the Spirit of God . . . [as] agent in creation . . . principle of life in all living things."† Central in the life in the community, so far as Christian experience goes, but also more widely, indeed cosmically at work, the Spirit now becomes one of the three ways in which Christians meet and know God: as the Father who sent Jesus Christ, in the Christ whom the Father sent, and in the fellowship which exists as the response of persons to Christ whom the Father sent. Here is the beginning of the development of the doctrine of the Godhead as triunitarian, a doctrine which is not a merely speculative effort on the part of theologians but a serious attempt to wrestle with what the "knowledge of God in Christ Jesus" and life in "the fellowship of the Spirit" must imply about the nature of God himself. Paul, in his famous Corinthians passage, puts that threefold yet unitary reality of Christian life in one phrase: "the grace of our Lord Jesus Christ, and the love of God, and the fellowship of the Holy Spirit."

In a very special sense, the working of the Spirit is seen in the process of "sanctification," through which the believer who is "justified by grace through faith" is increasingly conformed to Christ. This does not only mean growth in moral stature; it has to do with the deeper principle of life which is "in Christ" and which produces those moral fruits. We have so regularly identified "holiness" with ethical qualities that we have tended to forget that both in Judaism before Christ and in New Testament teaching after Christ's coming, holiness primarily indicated "belonging to God." It reminds us of the integral distinction between that which is God and of God and that which is not God. However difficult it may be to put this into words, the fact of the matter is clear enough. The Jewish people

* London: SCM Press, Ltd., 1969.
† Ibid., p. 326.

42

were said to be holy, not because they were extremely good (for they never claimed any such thing), but because they belonged to God and were his chosen instrument for effecting his will in the world. So also with the Christian fellowship. Members of Christ's Body were certainly expected to be good, reflecting in their lives the moral qualities manifested in Jesus himself; but they were members of that Body not because they were morally excellent but because they had been "called" to share the life which was "in Christ." That was what the possession of the Spirit meant in the first instance. Then the "fruits worthy of repentance" would appear in their attitudes and behavior, precisely because those who are "in Christ" are being "made holy" in the moral sense too. This order—first holiness as belonging to God, then holiness as moral goodness—is theologically stated when we speak *first* of "justification" and *then* of "sanctification."

It is not possible here to give a full account of the way in which the later theology of the church found place for the Holy Spirit in its doctrine of God. We can only summarize briefly some of the important aspects of that development. There can be no doubt that the datum with which that theology worked was triadic in nature. The very word trias was used in early days as a proper term to be applied to God.

The threefold quality of the original Christian conviction was *not* a matter of temporal succession but of the very reality of Christian life itself. Sometimes it has been said that first there was an awareness of Jahweh, the God of Israel. Then there was the appearance of Jesus, with all that this includes, and the sense that God was at work in him. And finally, there was the life of the Christian community, so conscious of a divine operation within it that its animating spirit must be the Spirit of God. Such a scheme of successive moments is not borne out by a consideration of the New Testament evidence nor of the way in which the early Christians thought. On the contrary, whatever may have been the situation before the coming of Jesus Christ, once that event had taken place there was immediately and by the very fact of his coming, a contemporaneous triadic quality in the meeting with and knowledge of God. God himself was in Christ so that to know Christ was at the same moment to know God. To know God in Christ was at the same moment to be "in the Spirit," for the immediacy and adequacy of the response to Christ was nothing other than the Spirit at work in the believer. Karl Barth, among others, has argued this point as against the "successive" view, and I believe that he has demonstrated its adequacy in relation to the New Testament evidence. Beyond the New Testament, the same point holds. The problem which the patristic age faced was *not* the discovery of a way in which three successive meetings with God, leading to threeness in what was said about God, could somehow be given unitary statement. It was exactly the reverse. The question was, "How can the one and only God be understood in such a fashion that each of the ways in which we have met him can be affirmed both as genuine in themselves and as somehow integral to that one and only God?" This was no experiential tritheism demanding a monotheistic expression; it was a stark and plain monotheism seeking a way in which the triadic experience of God-in-Christ-through-the-Spirit could somehow be preserved and validated.

The whole apparatus of theological terminology about Godhead results from this attempt of the Christian fathers to make sense of Christian life. Much of that language seems to us today to use overprecise distinctions: the processions, generations, filiations, etc., of which so much was made, appear to claim altogether too intimate a knowledge of what God is "in himself," as they would have put it. Nonetheless, what they were trying to do was something that had to be done, once the experience of life "in Christ" was taken as more than a human and subjective affair. If that life was in some very important manner an "opening" to people of the heart of the divinely worshipful reality called God, then the human experience of God must also be a reflection of what was true of God himself. Once again we see that triunitarian thinking is not the theorizing which might delight speculative minds; it is a serious effort to make sense of, give sense to, and properly interpret a vital reality of life which is the inescapable fact, the absolute heart and center, of Christianity.

At the end, the theological formulation which was adopted spoke about one God who is three *hypostases* yet one *ousia*.

Here we should do much better to retain the classical Greek terms, instead of attempting to put them into modern English. Even translation into Latin, beginning with Tertullian, was a perilous enterprise. Words have their connotations in the language in which they are originally found. The term *hypostasis* in Greek does not suggest the psychological elements which are inevitably present in the English word person. The Latin *persona* can suggest ideas not found in the Greek which it is supposed to translate. *Persona* was used in Latin to denote a legal entity. In modern English it denotes a "legal person," against whom a process of law might be initiated, to whom property belongs, etc. It also denoted the mask worn by an actor in a theatrical performance (as when we say *dramatis personae*, the "roles" played by the actress in a drama). Neither of these notions is adequate to *hypostasis*. How should we understand that Greek term? After much discussion and discrimination, the Cappadocians came to use it as signifying an abiding or eternal mode both of being and action. They were not talking about "centers of consciousness," as we do when we say person.

Much the same problem of translation and interpretation is attached to the Greek *ousia*. Basically it stands for "what this or that is *in itself*." It is distinguished from *phusis* (which we translate as nature) in that the latter signified for the Greek fathers "what a thing *is* in terms of what it *does*." To translate *ousia* into Latin as *substantia* or even as *essentia* was to suggest a variety of connotations from the Latin which can be highly misleading. To put *ousia* into English as substance is almost bound to make us think of some static or inert thing rather than a living and dynamic reality. And this is still true despite the efforts of centuries of theologians and philosophers to eradicate that "thing" quality from the meaning given to the term. Similarly with *essentia* put into English as essence. The proof of the difficulty is seen when Thomas Aquinas, struggling to retain a genuinely living quality in deity as against the implications of Aristotelian idiom, felt obliged to employ for God in himself the definition *esse a se subsistens* ("being subsisting from itself only"), and the notion of *aseitas* (or "being that is from itself alone") as the root-attribute of God. It becomes even worse when in pre-Kantian thought God is styled *ens realissimum* ("most real being") for here the neuter noun ens is bound to suggest to us in the starkest way a thing rather than the dynamism and vitality which in Jewish theology was taken to be the truth about God.

There is much to be said for the distinction made by Gregory Palamas, the later Greek theologian, between the divine essence and the divine energies. Here is the hint of the distinction which Whitehead made between God as "primordial" (and hence abstract and eternal) and God as "consequent" (and hence concrete and everlasting). What is significant in Palamas' use of the terms is that the divine essence is not separate and different from the energies. The energies, or God's attributes as his working, are identical with God as he essentially is; but his "essence" is that mysterious quality of God which is behind and beyond what he is known in his world to "do." Something like that is still useful to us in our formulation of a viable concept of God, provided that we do not fall into the error of doing what Whitehead called "paying God metaphysical compliments" by putting the primary stress on that which is "beyond and behind" rather than on that which is disclosed in act. For as all the fathers understood perfectly, whatever God is is given in and disclosed by what he does. His very character as God is his self-giving love. The mystery is in the inexhaustible, indefatigable, indefeasible, boundless quality of that love, beyond anything we can envisage or understand.

The last few pages may have seemed to have little direct relation to our theme of the Holy Spirit. But they were not a departure from that subject; they were a necessary preliminary to an understanding of what the formalized doctrine of the Spirit is really saying. And what is that?

The doctrine is an assertion that the Spirit is absolutely and truly divine, in exactly the sense in which the Father and the eternal Word or Son or Logos are divine. Through a long struggle, including its Arian phase when the Word was a "created divine," and the later phase when the Word was fully divine but the Spirit was secondarily or derivately divine, the patristic age came at last to its affirmation of the three *hypostases* in one *ousia*. This led to a further difference of opinion as to the models which might best be used to grasp what was intended. One model used the analogy of human relationships and the other model that of human psychological distinctions.

In the former instance, found in one place in the *De Trinitate* of Augustine, we may speak of Father, Son, and Spirit, as Lover, the Beloved who loves in return, and the Love which is the bond between them. Basil of Caesarea, one of the great Cappadocian theologians, could take as an analogy "Peter, James, and John," knit together in the oneness of humanity. What is frequently forgotten by modern theologians* is the Platonic world-view of the Cappadocians and of Augustine. For a Platonist, the basic realities are precisely the forms or ideas in which appearances or visible phenomena participate. Hence for Basil the three men, Peter and James and John, are *not* the basic reality; rather the basic reality is the manhood which they all share as men. For Augustine, the Lover, the Beloved, and the Love which binds them together, are not discrete and separable entities basically real in themselves; what is basically real is the indefinable "lovingness" in which they all participate. Hence the analogy of relationships used in the patristic writings does not suggest anything tritheistic. In Thomas Aquinas, who also used the relationship analogy, the monotheism of the concept becomes crystal clear.

In respect to the psychological analogy, we find this also in Augustine, who more consistently speaks of memory, understanding, and will (or elsewhere of mind, knowledge, and love, and of other similar sets of three), as a way of understanding the Godhead. In a man, for example, there is the unadulterated awareness which he styles *memoria*, the understanding or *intellectus* which is operational awareness, and the *voluntas* or will which effects whatever is known and then returns reflexively to pure awareness as the consciousness of that effect. Obviously the analysis is subtle; in terms of the kind of psychology which Augustine believed valid, it is useful enough. But for us the psychology is out-of-date. One reason for this is that through building on Augustine's own introspective thought, later psychological understanding was bound to go beyond it (quite apart

* In particular the Anglican writers who have made much of what they call "the social analogy." Leonard Hodgson's *Doctrine of the Trinity* is a book which particularly stresses this analogy.

47

from more recent experimental and "depth" psychological work). We can hardly be content with the analogy. Nonetheless, it is still suggestive in at least one sense; it makes quite clear to us that here again the monotheistic stress was primary, for Augustine in his very use of the analogy strongly insists on *una mens* (one mind) as inclusive of the three "factors" to which he points.

In the social analogy, God the Spirit is love; in the psychological analogy he is will. In both the Spirit is "he." This brings us to the problem which is usually styled "the personality of the Spirit." How can the "bond of love" be personal in the same sense in which Father and Son may be seen as such? How can will be personal at all? Is it not an activity of persons, rather than itself personal?

But here we must recall that the term *hypostasis* in the Greek Fathers did not carry with it the highly personalistic psychology which we associate with the English notion of person or personality. The intention was not to talk of "personal centers of consciousness" nor of the kind of psychological process (in its relatively high degree of integration) which we indicate when we use the word person. A good deal of recent formal theological discussion of person and personality in God, as well as talk of God himself as a person, rests upon a misunderstanding of the patristic view. For the fathers, God was most certainly not conceived as *three things* which somehow are *one thing*. That absurdity was never in their minds. But neither did they conceive of God as three district foci of psychological consciousness or awareness who somehow make up one personal being. They could not have thought in that way, and their formulae should not be read in that way.*

Perhaps Augustine was wisest when he remarked in the *De Trinitate* that we say "three persons because we must not be silent" about God. And perhaps the tendency in other writers of the time to say "the three" rather than "three persons" (or the Greek equivalent) was an instance of humility and care in speaking. However we may think, the fact remains that the

---

* G. L. Prestige to the contrary notwithstanding. Compare his discussion in *God in Patristic Thought* (Naperville, Ind.: Alec R. Allenson, Inc., 1952) and *Fathers and Heretics* (Allenson, 1940).

fathers were prepared to insist that whatever divinity may seem appropriate to ascribe to Father and Son (or Word) is equally appropriate in respect to the Spirit. His divinity or Godhead was taken to be identical with what was meant when this was attributed to Father and Son. Presumably one ground for this insistence was in the highly personalizing experience of the Spirit's activity in the life of the Christian believer and in the worship and work of the Christian community. We need not pursue the matter at this point. In the final chapter, when we attempt to speak more fully of the Christian triunitarian portrayal of God, we shall return to the issue of person and personality.

Finally, we must comment briefly on the patristic refusal to confine the Spirit and his working to the individual Christian or to the Christian church. Origen, almost alone among the Fathers, appears to have thought that the Holy Spirit is not only specifically and decisively, but exclusively known in the response made personally and socially in Christian faith to the activity of the Word or Logos or Son in Jesus Christ. But the general tendency in the patristic age was to recognize the Spirit elsewhere as well. Certainly in the older dispensation of Israel as they would have thought of it, the Spirit was both present and at work. They did not reject the Old Testament and its witness to the Spirit among the Jews and in the life and worship of the Jewish people. Furthermore, what Dr. Haroutunian called the "cosmic" aspect of the Spirit's working was very much in their thought, although its implications were not spelled out in any detail or with any precision.

In much the same way as the eternal Word of God, the Logos or Son was distinctively and specifically incarnate in Jesus Christ at a given time and place in history (yet was also the same Word whose *organon* was the whole creation, as Athanasius affirms in the *De Incarnatione*), so also the Spirit was peculiarly and decisively known in the Christian life, as members of Christ were "sanctified" and the community which was the Body of Christ was enabled to work and pray and adore. But the Spirit was not only there. He was everywhere in the creation; his universal operation was linked up with the activity of the Word; and it was by him that the Word was received and given the response which was demanded when he was seen for what he was and for what he did. There was a generosity of mind here which we shall do well to emulate, even as we shall also do well to enlarge it and apply it to areas to which the Fathers themselves never did, or did only by vague suggestion and intimation.

In this chapter we have been content with a very swift survey of the material found in scripture and of the developments made by the early theology of the church in the light of the difference which the coming of Jesus was bound to make in the vision of God and his ways in the world. In the next chapter we shall build on this discussion. In that chapter we shall move on to a simpler, much less technical treatment. We shall ask what is meant for us today when in creedal language we affirm of the Spirit that he is "Lord," and go on to speak of him as "the Giver of Life."

4

The Lord,
the Life-giver

"... and I believe in the Holy Ghost, the Lord, the Giver of life, who proceedeth from the Father [and the Son], who with the Father and the Son together is worshipped and glorified, who spake by the prophets."

These are very familiar words to those of us who are accustomed to attend with regularity the celebration of the Holy Communion. They are at the very heart of the creed we repeat together, and they are used by Christians of all types and denominations (save that the Eastern Orthodox are more loyal to the original form of that creed and omit the three words we have placed in brackets). We shall have something to say about those words, the *filioque*, in a later part of this chapter.

We do indeed repeat these phrases about the Holy Spirit, and it is regrettable that because of the use of the word ghost in the English idiom of the age when the *Book of Common Prayer* was compiled (and later in the King James or Authorized Version of the Bible, too), the impression is given to the uninstructed that we are talking about some eerie spectral being. We repeat these phrases, but what do we think they mean? The purpose of this chapter is to state, as simply and clearly as possible, what we are talking about when we speak of him who is called in the creed "the Lord, the Giver of life." And incidently it is worth observing, before we begin, that the creedal form which is found in the 1662 English Prayer Book gives a mistaken impression by saying "the Lord and Giver of life." The sense of those words suggests that the Holy Spirit is the Lord of life *and* the Giver of life. Neither the Greek original of the creed nor its Latin translation, both of them naturally earlier than our English text, bears out this idea. Rather they make it clear that in calling the Spirit "Lord" the intention is to affirm his true divinity as one to be "worshipped and glorified." Furthermore, the "Lord of life" is Jesus Christ as the signal self-disclosure of God the Father. The Spirit is indeed divine; he is also the One who "gives" or "brings" life to those to whom he comes. That is the point of the phrase; that is why the Spirit is styled "Life-giver."

Now this creedal affirmation is a summing up in capsule form, as we might put it, of the overall witness of the New Testament and the primitive Christian interpretation of that witness. When it speaks of the Holy Spirit it is referring to a very central part of that witness and interpretation. It is speaking of a real fact of experience, which Christians believe to be also a real experience. Yet of all the articles in the creed, it is probable that this one about the Spirit is for many Christian people the vaguest, the most obscure, perhaps the most meaningless in terms of rational understanding. Certainly it is one that makes very little sense to those who are outside the Christian church.

There is no problem when we use the word spirit with a lowercase *s*. It is easy to see what is intended when we speak of "the spirit of Britain," "the spirit of America," "the British spirit," "the American spirit." But when we capitalize spirit and speak of "Holy Spirit" we begin to have trouble. On the other hand, it may very well be the case, as Canon T. O. Wedel remarked in one of his books, that through consideration of our meaning when we say "the British spirit" or "the American spirit" we can begin to grasp what is meant by "Holy Spirit." Very shortly we shall undertake this approach. But here it is important to stress the centrality of the Spirit in all Christian experience and thought; even more, to stress the truth that if

Christian faith is true and if the Christian life is genuinely life in relation to God and people, the Holy Spirit is constantly with us and in us. Belief in him is utterly fundamental to a sound and basic Christian view of things.

Failure to recognize this fundamental character of the Holy Spirit in the Christian way, failure to have some understanding of who he is and what he does, is responsible for much that is false and wrong in our religious thinking. As we have said, it is the explanation of much of the confusion in people's minds about the significance of the church, for example, or about the manner in which the sacraments of the church are effectual and validated. It is also true that a failure to respond to the fact of the Spirit's presence and power has resulted in the impotence of much conventional Christianity. The recovery of the sense of his presence and power has been made in our own time by the Pentecostal sects which have become so strong in many parts of the world—not only among uneducated and primitive people, as is often incorrectly said, but also among sophisticated and intelligent ones. One can hope that this recovery, with the enthusiasm which accompanies it, will spread more widely, bringing about renewal of vitality like that which in English religious history the Wesleyan movement accomplished with its enthusiasm, based on a strong sense of the Spirit at work in people's lives and in the world.

We have noted that most of us are fairly sure what is meant when we hear the word spirit with a small s. The phrase "the spirit of Britain" expresses the binding together in a national unity of the people of England. Through loyalty to common ideals and aims, through participation in a common heritage, they share in that spirit. There is an impulse to work together for the general good, with patriotic awareness of all that Britain has stood for in the past and with recognition of the claims which Britain makes in the present. This common sharing may be at cost, even sacrificial cost, as when a subject of the Queen is called upon to lay down his life for his country, its way of life, its values, perhaps its very existence. "The spirit of Britain" can take possession of a man, compel him to act, urge him, persuade him, inspire him, even comfort him. During World War II, everybody realized this, often in a poignant way; and of that

53

spirit Winston Churchill was the great exemplar during times of terrible distress.

What was so clear with Churchill and this experience was the gracious quality of spirit, its social and embodied character, and its communication to those who are somehow admitted to the community where that spirit is shared. The "Holy Spirit" means much more than this; yet, as I have said, this may be a good place to start. Note that we have used the personal pronoun he, not the impersonal pronoun it, in referring to the Holy Spirit. That is one point of difference: the "spirit of Britain" is "it," but the Holy Spirit is "he." Why? Primarily because the Spirit does not coerce or force or exert pressure in an impersonal way, but also because the Spirit (as Christian experience shows) effects in those to whom he comes a personalizing of their lives in a highly specific sense, making them "persons in Christ," integrating them in conscious allegiance to Christ, sharpening their sense of selfhood precisely in enabling them to lose superficial and unworthy aspects of self in such allegiance. The Spirit is not known as a vague, diffused, subpersonal, or mechanical influence. None of those objectives will serve. He is active, energizing, living, focused in his work, acting personally in human life. One could not say all that about the spirit of Britain. This is where the analogy breaks down, useful as it is.

On the other hand, there are many things which may be said about the Holy Spirit which are not unlike the statements we may make about spirit with the lowercase s. Let us refer to the early Christian community for further understanding of this matter.

Jesus Christ had come among people, teaching, preaching, healing, and performing "mighty acts." He had gathered around him a band of followers who companied with him. He had attacked the perversions of Jewish religion as he saw them in the leaders of his people. He had therefore been arrested, tried, and crucified. And he had manifested himself after his death to his disciples through "many infallible proofs." This complex of happenings was summed up in what we call the "event of Christ." But what was the response to this event in its fullness? The answer is given in the whole of the New Testament, including Gospels and the letters and that strange visionary book known

54

as "the Revelation of St. John the Divine." The impact or impression of this event was such that the disciples and those whom they won to their fellowship found themselves possessed by a new spirit. It will be observed that for the present we content ourselves with the lowercase *s*, since we are talking about a phenomenon which resembles the kind of spirit we talk about when we speak of "the spirit of a school." So there was this new spirit; the spirit was one of common belonging to the fellowship; it signified the togetherness of believer with believers. The spirit brought with it an empowering or strengthening of those possessed by it, so that they became bold people—so bold that the authorities were surprised by the attitude of such simple and uneducated people and could only conclude that "they had been with Jesus," whose boldness had been so marked and extraordinary in the face of Jewish priests and Roman officials. Above all, the spirit was characterized by love, especially manifested within the little company itself but also shown in a desire to help and heal those outside that band of Christian believers.

Yet there was the difference which makes the analogy inadequate. For this spirit known to the Christians and seen in the Christian fellowship was so remarkably authoritative and compelling in its quality, so demanding of obedience to the Lord whom the Christian company served, so insistent in persuasive action within them, and so unexpectedly effective in empowering enthusiastic and wholehearted discipleship, that the experience recalled Joel's words about the pouring out of God's Spirit upon all flesh. Furthermore, as we noted, the action of the spirit was personalizing rather than destructive of the personal quality in each of the believers. As personalizing the Spirit must be conceived personally. Hence there was no talk about spirit as a vague influence; the talk was about *the* Spirit, the Spirit of God himself. The Spirit, identified with the Spirit about whom they had read in their scriptures (which were of course the Jewish collection of sacred books), was the Spirit who had come mightily upon men of old, the Spirit by whom God had spoken to the prophets of the old dispensation. This was the Spirit "who sweetly ordereth all things," who is the vividly felt presence and power of God in men's hearts, in historical events, and in the sustaining of the natural orders.

55

The interpretation was inevitable, granted the background of Judaism with which the first Christians were so familiar. The Spirit who was given to this band of believers in the risen Lord was the Spirit who not only was experienced by each member of the company. Much more than that, he was the Spirit who filled the church, the community itself, with his presence and who was seen and known to be working in that church by his power. He was the Spirit *of Christ,* since (as the writer of John's Gospel saw) he "took of the things of Christ"—what Christ had said and done—"and declared them," made them come alive, for those who shared in Christ's Body. His gifts were precisely those qualities which the memory of Christ in the church's proclamation and teaching identified as characteristic of the Lord himself in the "days of his flesh." The "fruit of the Spirit" was identical with the impression which Jesus had made—here was love, joy, peace, long-suffering, kindness, temperance—positive virtues which were not produced by hard moral struggle toward perfection but received as by grace or gift. This was the Spirit of God,.come from God, given through Christ, received by those who lived in the fellowship of the church.

In his *Common Life in the Body of Christ,* Lionel Thornton portrayed this "new existence" which was specifically known as Christian in the first days of the church. Surveying the whole range of New Testament material, he showed how fresh and strong that existence was, how it was related to the life of the community, and how it took possession of each Christian believer. He also showed how what happened had forced people to use their minds. What could all this mean? The more reflective members of the church could not rest content simply with the experience which they knew; they were obliged to think about it. As they did so, they began the interpretative process which did not finish, in formal theological terms, until several centuries later. As with the belief in Christ himself, it took time to think out and think through the significance of what was known. Indeed it took longer for the doctrine of the Spirit to be given some formal statement, for the simple reason that the Holy Spirit is primarily a reality lived and experienced, not a problem set for people to solve. But it was right that theologians should attempt to place this reality in its divine content, not by treating the reality as a "problem" but rather as a "given" with which the mind must wrestle.

Any faith which is to be acceptable must in the long run give an account of itself; any experience which is not to be dismissed as illusory must be filled in with other experiences and placed in some coherent setting. This is what Christian theologians did in respect to the Holy Spirit and his working in the world. In the remainder of this chapter we shall summarize briefly what they came to say, not in the precise theological terms discussed in the last chapter but in the experiential terms of Christian life. The reason for our making this kind of summary may be found in the observation which we have made on two previous occasions: The Christian theological enterprise, more particularly when it treats of God and his activity, is not a speculative game, but a serious effort to interpret given facts as these have been experienced and lived by men and women in the Christian church. Whenever this has been forgotten and mere theorizing has taken over, the result has been an arid and ultimately irrelevant exercise which is often more damaging to true religion and real faith than anything else that good people may do.

First of all, then, Christian thought has said that the Holy Spirit is Lord. That is stated plainly in the creedal formulation which we quoted at the beginning of this chapter. To call the Holy Spirit "Lord" means to call him worthy of worship—that is to say, divine. No Christian would have thought of worshiping anything or anyone not truly divine; the refusal to make even a symbolic gesture of veneration to the Roman emperor's statue, for example, had led many Christians in the time of persecution to suffer death as martyrs. But to say "divine" was also to say *God*. If there is only one worshipful reality who may be called divine, that reality is God himself, the supreme and perfect One revealed in Jesus Christ as righteousness and love.

A modern writer, Charles Williams, has written of "our Lord the Holy Spirit." This is a useful phrase, for it reminds us that in Christian thinking the Holy Spirit is not a "stepped-down" or depotentiated divinity. There had been some Christians who had thought in this way, as we saw in the chapter on theological development, but they were outreasoned by other Christians and their view was rejected as heretical. It was a deviation from the orthodox or sound-thinking position because essential elements in the Christian life were either imperiled or denied by such opinions. Just as the Arian theology, which had a somewhat similar stepped-down notion of the Eternal Word who was incarnate in Jesus, had been shown to be impossible through the efforts of Athanasius and others a century before, so the depotentiation of the Holy Spirit was declared to be an impossible view. The Holy Spirit was declared to be true God.

Naturally this was not an easy position to take, for it aggravated the whole problem of the nature of Godhead. How could the Holy Spirit be truly God, if the Father is God and the Eternal Word or Son is also God? The unity of the Godhead, which is to say the strict monotheism which the Christian church inherited from Judaism, seemed threatened, first by ascription of true deity to the Word or Son, and now by the ascription of that same true deity to the Holy Spirit. The difficulty was real; but the Fathers of the Christian church were prepared to have it before them rather than to deny an indubitable reality in the Christian life in grace. Thus the stage was set for the working out, in however difficult form, of the doctrine of the Triunity of Godhead. Of this we have already spoken; we shall return to it in the last chapter of this book.

The Holy Spirit is true God. But second, the Holy Spirit is the responsive agency in Godhead. We shall also return to this in the closing chapter. Here we need only note that while the theologians of the first five or six centuries of the church did not put their conviction in just those words, their intention was plainly to assert what we have just said. This powerful energizing, known in the hearts and wills and desires of Christian people, known even more in the binding together of all believers in the unity of the Christian fellowship, was none other than God's power of love which awakened in the faithful a response of adoration, obedience, and love toward God for what he had accomplished in history in the event of Jesus Christ. But if that response in the faithful was to be validated as more than a merely subjective feeling—and of this the Christian community was utterly convinced—then in some fashion response must be found also in the Godhead himself. The Holy Spirit was God, but he was God in a "responsive mode," as we would phrase it in our own idiom. The eternal God both wills responsive love and includes responsive love. Indeed he *is* responsive love. Here once again the triunitarian conception of God is plainly implied. For while the Father is the source or principle of the creative process, the "maker of all things," unfathomable in his mystery; and while the Eternal Word or Son is the self-expression of God both in the creation and in the heart of the deity, the outgoing which reveals and manifests the Father for what truly the Father is in himself; so also the Holy Spirit is the "responding," the conforming, the returning or the "amen" of God through the whole creation and in deity itself. The circle is made complete: God is self-expressive; God is self-responsive.

There are difficulties here of which perhaps the patristic age was not sufficiently aware. It was working with the categories of Greek and later Latin (modified by Greek) thought. For reasons which we shall see, these categories were not able to contain the fundamentally Jewish-Christian position that God is always creative and, perhaps more significantly, always related. Hence the circle really cannot be closed. Somehow it must be a circle open to the world in which God's creativity is always at work and with which God is unfailingly related. But at the time, the ancient theologians did the best they could be expected to do. They preserved the reality and validity of the Christian data; they formulated a view which was at least coherent, even if not entirely adequate to all that the data required. And they went on to say that in respect to the world, the Holy Spirit "proceeds" from the Father *through* the Son. That is, the responsive movement is preparatory for, stimulated by, and answers to the work of the eternal Word wherever that Word is operative. We have stressed the preposition through because unhappily the Western Church, centering its attention especially on some New Testament phrases and realizing that Jesus had been for Christians the proximate source of the Spirit in their experience, put into the creed the phrase about the Spirit "proceeding from the Father *and* the Son." By doing this, they alienated the more careful thinkers of the Eastern Church whose theology had been more precise in thinking, if not always in saying, that the Father was always the true source, while it was "through" the eternal Word that he "sent forth" the Spirit to be the response. Of that "throughness" the specific "sending" of the Spirit by Jesus was, so to say, the decisive instance. Yet it was in fact not so much *by* Jesus as *through* him and his coming that the Spirit was given.

The Spirit, then, "proceeds" from the Father through the Son, with all that the Son manifests and achieves; and the Spirit returns to the Father. For the patristic age, it is like a closed circle, we have said. Yet in fairness to the fathers the circle is not completely closed, even for them, because into it all that has been made by God and done by God and disclosed of God, with its consequences, is brought back to God, perfected and made more and more adequately by God's own through the action of the Spirit by whom it is thus returned.

Third, the theologians of the church were insistent that the Holy Spirit was not interested only in the Christian fellowship and in matters of a religious sort. He was indeed the "Giver of life," and of *all* life, wherever and however found; more than that, he was discoverable in the entire created order, in its every range. (To this we shall give fuller attention in the following chapter.) The drive through the natural order, for example, by which it conforms to some intentional pattern, was for Christian theologians who built on the patristic affirmations nothing other than the hidden working of the Holy Spirit. One might put it in graphic modern terms by saying that it is he who in a mysterious fashion, not visible to scientific observation and not as a strange additional entelechy either, makes the acorn grow into an oak tree. It is he who is the reason for a child's movement to adulthood and for a person's fulfillment of one's potentialities. The Holy Spirit is not life in the biological sense, of course. That would be absurd, and for the Christian theologians, would also be a mistakenly pantheistic notion. Rather, he is the Spirit in and behind life, the Spirit "who makes things grow" and who sees to it that "things make themselves."

As a consequence of this, and as our fourth point in summary of the development of Christian thought about the Spirit, it was clear that the Holy Spirit speaks, works, and moves in all sorts of unexpected and secular places. Since he is everywhere, he is also active everywhere. One immediate implication should be pointed out. If the Holy Spirit is in and behind what goes on in the world, nobody need be afraid of new truth wherever it is seen, new discoveries whatever they may be, new ideas however odd they may appear to be. His action is in one sense veiled, so that it is not at once recognized for what it is. But it is there; and a responsibility of the Christian is to see this and acknowledge it.

When D. H. Lawrence the novelist, poet, and agnostic (so far as Christian faith was concerned), wrote that he did not feel that his verse was produced by himself alone but in some fashion by what he styled "the wind that bloweth through me," he was testifying (albeit unconsciously) to what Christians mean when they speak of the life-giving power of the Holy Spirit, the Spirit who inspires men to speak truth, create beauty, serve, and do good. Wherever such goodness, truth, righteousness, and beauty are present and demand assent, the Holy Spirit is hiddenly and anonymously at work. Or, to take another illustration, we may recall how Vincent van Gogh said that when he arrived in Arles, after his years in the darkened mining villages of Belgium, he felt an inward compulsion to paint bright yellow sunlight. Why and how this compulsion came, he said he did not know. But so strong was this compulsion, he told his brother Theo, that he was at length bound to yield to it—and so we get those brilliant paintings which seem suffused with the light of the sun. A Christian ought to see that if one follows the implications of the doctrine of the Holy Spirit as the Christian theologians worked it out, the Holy Spirit was working in van Gogh. And again, when persons are bound together in community through dedication to a compelling cause or ideal which is truly good, the Holy Spirit is operative in the spirit which makes them such a community, provided that the spirit is in fact "upbuilding," constructive, and for the common good.

It ought to be the duty as it is the privilege of Christians to recognize and affirm the manifold and mysterious working throughout the creation, in human history, and in human experience, of the Spirit who "ordereth all things" and who brings about a response to good in any form in which it appears. The cosmic sweep of the Spirit's operation is a truth that greatly needs

61

recovery in Christian circles, prone as those circles are to parochialize the Spirit and to attempt to confine him to religious or ecclesiastical channels.

Nonetheless we must not unduly minimize those channels, because it is through them—in the broadest sense, with no automatism or mechanical working—that the conscious awareness of the Spirit has become most apparent to believers. This is the fifth and last point in this summary. The theologians of the church have affirmed with sure conviction that the Holy Spirit is the Spirit of the church, its living power of response to God in Christ, who guides the Christian fellowship into more and more of the truth as it is in Jesus. Here we make our contact with Canon Wedel's point in the discussion of spirit earlier in this chapter.

The Holy Spirit makes Jesus a reality in the Christian's experience. When I was a child I was taught a rather "high church" catechism, one part of which ran, "What does the Holy Spirit do?" with the answer, "He makes Jesus present still." That answer is a brief summary of what the theologians of the church said in the early days of Christianity. The Spirit makes Jesus present by awakening in people the capacity to receive the "grace of our Lord Jesus Christ," thus conforming them to "the image of the Son." He works constantly through the fellowship of the faithful, with all their failure and error and sin, to bring the riches of God in Christ into the lives of people wherever they may be. The "fruit of the Spirit" is released into and through the church; individual lives, shaped and molded in the "fellowship of the Holy Spirit," reflect the love, joy, peace, long-suffering, meekness, and temperance which are the very qualities that were present vividly and compellingly in Jesus, to whom (as the New Testament puts it) "the Spirit was given without measure." The Holy Spirit, who is Lord and thus divine, who is Life-giver, indwells the church and makes it become the church. As people obediently respond to God by him and through him, as he authoritatively yet without coercive force takes possession of their lives, and as he conforms them to the pattern of Christ, he becomes a vital reality. In worship, above all, and especially in the Lord's Supper or eucharist, the Spirit effects the sacramental oblation and presence, making simple bread and wine "holy things" which people may eat "in the presence of [God's] divine majesty."

Nobody and nothing can escape the presence and the power of God the Holy Spirit; this is a given of the Christian experience of life "in Christ." Sometimes the presence and power are known in gentle ways, sometimes in apparently overwhelming possession, but always by persuasion rather than by coercive force. For Christian faith it is in the church's fellowship that people share in the fullest sense in the reality of the Spirit's activity. And what is that activity within the fellowship of the Spirit? It is the *in*-forming of people in community in such a fashion that they are *con*-formed to Christ, who is the Lord of life.

5

The Spirit at Work in the World

We begin, of set purpose, with a consideration of the Holy Spirit in his cosmic and historical activity. In this way we may be able to do something to counteract the inveterate tendency of so many Christians to parochialize and ecclesiasticize the Spirit of God, making him seem so often only a function of the religious aspect of human experience. The very real and important working of the Spirit in the church and in people's individual existence is never to be forgotten, but it can be properly understood only when it is seen in the context of the more universal working with which we shall concern ourselves in this chapter. In other words, to adopt an Americanism, we need "to take the big view"; then the personal and churchly immediacy of the Spirit's operation will be seen in the right way, and our proportions will be sound and true.

We may begin by a quotation from Leonard Hodgson's study of the doctrine of the Trinity, in his book by that name. In one place Dr. Hodgson writes:

Think, for example, of the doctor confronted by some difficult problem of diagnosis. He has behind him years of training in the medical schools, enriched by subsequent experience in clinical practice, together with the continued study of the literature of his science and discussion with fellow-physicians. All these together, working it may be upon the basis of a certain natural gift, have gone to make him the man he is, the kind of man prepared in a crisis to receive the flash of illumination whereby he sees the true explanation of the patient's unfamiliar condition. The Christian interpretation of this wide-spread element in human experience is that in every such occurrence we have an instance of the working of the Spirit of God.*

Professor Hodgson's words splendidly sum up the point which we wish to make, and they link with some other words of his in the same book:

We must not forget . . . that God who makes himself known to us in our Christian faith is the same God who is at work throughout his universe. So far from leading us to deny the value of non-Christian thought, our faith should enable us to recognize the activity of God in confronting, correcting, and straightening the vision of men, even when they themselves are unaware of the source of their enlightenment.†

So the Spirit of God is everywhere at work, leading men to respond to truth wherever it is found and to receive from God that which he wills to disclose in any place. To see things in this way is to be delivered from narrowness and pettiness in our religious life. To accept this vision and live in its light is to discover a freshness and joy which redeems daily existence from the triviality and superficiality which all too often seems inescapable and frustrating.

In the Prayer Book of the American Episcopal Church there is an "invitatory" intended to precede the recitation of the *Venite* at Morning Prayer on Whitsunday, the traditional festival which in the Christian church calendar commemorates the

* Leonard Hodgson, *The Doctrine of the Trinity* (London: Nisbet and Co., Ltd., 1943), pp. 40-41.
† Ibid., pp. 138-39.

"gift of the Holy Spirit" to the disciples at the Feast of Pentecost. The words of the invitatory are as follows:

Alleluia. The Spirit of the Lord filleth the world:
O come, let us adore him. Alleluia.

Words like that are the charter for the wider operation of the Spirit with which we are concerned here. They serve to make clear that it is not enough to *say* the activity of God the Holy Spirit is cosmic in sweep, and then immediately proceed to *think of him* as confined to the church itself or to religious matters. We have admitted that the Spirit is supremely and distinctively known in the church which is "the followship of the Holy Spirit" and in the experience of personal conformation to the image of Christ. But we have gone on to say that there is more than that.

Perhaps one reason that the wide and generous working of the Holy Spirit is not always understood is to be found in the fact that he is indeed, as my old teacher remarked, "the most modest 'Person' of the Godhead." Generally he prefers to work incognito. He does not proclaim himself; rather, he operates through the whole creation to bring it to its intended perfection by conforming it to the perfect plan of God manifest humanly in Jesus Christ. He works to return all things to their Creator, fulfilled and perfected as they more and more become obedient to that Creator's will. Despite his anonymity, however, the Holy Spirit is there. The Christian who is informed about the meaning of faith should know that the creation cannot properly be understood apart from the Spirit of the Lord "who filleth the world."

This very anonymity, however, creates a difficulty for us. We are in danger of identifying some particular natural event or historical occurrence as so much the work of the Holy Spirit that we fail to attend to the causes in the natural order or in the realm of historical happening which are open to our investigation and with which science and historical enquiry should deal. Our illustration of the acorn and oak can show how this mistake may take place. It is quite possible for someone who has been brought to recognize the activity of the Spirit in the process by which the acorn grows up into an oak tree, to forget altogether that from the strictly scientific point of view, interested only in natural linkages of cause and effect, there is a description which is entirely valid so far as it goes and which will tell us how from that point of view the acorn becomes the oak tree. Here in that forgetfulness is an example of that confusion of categories to which we alluded earlier in this book. Alternatively, it is possible for someone to assume that the notion of the Holy Spirit is quite gratuitous in this connection. After all, it may be said, the scientific description is adequate for our scientific purposes, so why introduce the Spirit at all? Here we have not so much a confusion of categories as satisfaction with proximate explanations which by their very nature leave out of the picture the ultimate reason for there being any processive movement at all, any ground upon which the creative advance may be understood, and any way of seeing how novelty emerges out of continuity and how continuity goes forward without chaos.

To discover how God works in his creation is not to say that he does not work there. This we ought to have grasped when we finally accepted the evolutionary theory as the proper account of the mode of the divine creation of the world. But our imagination can fail us. We can limit ourselves to reporting what happens in that evolutionary movement as if it explained itself in an ultimate sense, or we can introduce the activity of God as if a deus ex machina intruded from some supposed outside into the created world. But where would that outside be? To ask that is to see the silliness of the notion, just as to suppose that sequence of cause and effect is all there is to the world demonstrates our incapacity to wrestle effectively with the ultimate mystery of the creation as a whole.

In the natural order, then, God the Spirit is at work. The invisible pressure in the world, moving in every created entity from whirling electron to the mind of the human, urging each entity to become that which it was intended to be—but urging it anonymously, through the subtlety of order and through the presentation of lure—is the work of the Word and of the Holy Spirit of God. Each entity is given its initial aim, each entity is surrounded by other entities which it may grasp and by which it may be grasped, and each entity is invited or lured to the pattern of its proper perfection. What is the final reason for this? Here the Christian will dare to say that this reason is "the Spirit of the Lord who filleth the world."

At the level of what is commonly known as the inorganic, where there is no conscious awareness and even no really living matter, as the phrase has it, the Holy Spirit is yet at work in establishing whatever perfection is proper to that level. But the word inorganic is not the correct one since the whole world is in fact a series of organisms of greater or less complexity—even the electron is correctly interpreted only when seen as a very low-grade "society." We have in the world no mere "matter-in-motion," as the nineteenth-century mechanistic physicists would have said; we have social patterns of an organic type, each element with its own aim, each with its own prehensions, each with its own goal. The Spirit holds all this together in an ongoing process. Furthermore, the Spirit works subtly to bring about such configurations and novel patterns as shall provide for the possibility of the emergence of further and higher levels in the creation.

As our observation leads us up the scale, more and more of the Spirit's work is seen in the living and conscious levels or grades or dimensions of the cosmos. At last we come to the sphere of history and the realm of human personality with conscious awareness of freedom of decision. Looking back from that point, we are then enabled to get an idea of what the Holy Spirit is after; it is the free surrender of the creation to what God purposes for it. Nor is this surrender, freely decided upon, an abrogation of the integrity of each occasion. Precisely and exactly in becoming truly *itself*, that which it has the possibility of becoming, the occasion obeys the will of God. Thus this divine will is not alien to the advance of the world, as some people would seem to think, for one hears them talk of interposition, intrusion, or violation of the order of nature and use all the rest of the words associated with the common meaning given to the miraculous. From our point of view, however, the self-realization of the given entities *is* the will of God for those entities, provided we see that self-realization means genuine fulfillment and not a deviant or distorted version of realization. Miracle is not an intrusive disturbing of the continuity with the novelties that appear within it; miracle is the actual presence and power of God in a particular occasion, as people come clearly to see this presence and power through the eye of faith.

As we shall observe in another chapter, the specific operation of the Spirit in the Christian fellowship is rightly interpreted as the disclosure in special clarity of what God the Spirit is *always* "up to" in the world. There we can say that it is all a matter of Love at work in the world. And it is the Christian privilege, entirely unmerited by those who enjoy it, to be taken into that Love and used by it so that people may become as it were "the priests of creation," offering it, in their own response to God the Father as Love, through the power of the Holy Spirit. But in the natural order of things, as the orthodox theologian Francis J. Hall once pointed out, the particular way in which the Holy Spirit reveals his working is through the ordered harmony and beauty of the world. We do not pay anything like sufficient attention to this, although the phrase about the Spirit "who sweetly ordereth all things" should have taught us this fact. And in a very serious sense the Holy Spirit is the Spirit of beauty —not with a small s, as if we were talking about how lovely a carnation seems to us, but with a capital S, for we are talking about the divine Spirit who so moves in the creation that harmony is achieved, loveliness comes into being (including that manifested in the incarnation), and human eyes are enabled to see and appreciate the harmony and loveliness wherever it is visible. The range of such harmony and beauty includes the orderly movement of the stars, the regularity and variety in the infinitesimal charges of energy in the submicroscopic electron, the color of a flower, the glory of a sunset, the beauty of a human face, and much else.

One is conscious that to speak in this fashion may arouse in some the charge of sentimentalism or the accusation of confusing what appears to us as attractive with what is actually there in the world outside us. But to think in these ways would be a mistake. What apppears to us as characterized by harmony and beauty has some relationship with phenomena which we observe. Many philosophers writing of aesthetics have noted that the value judgments people make in these ways presuppose a relationship of some sort between the human mind and the

69

observable external thing. But the real tragedy is the tendency of many good people to underestimate the importance of beauty in order to exalt the importance of goodness or righteousness. I wish to urge with all my force that the aesthetic, in the serious sense of that word, is not merely a matter of human fancy but is a response to what is really there in the world. The sheer glory found in so much of nature—granted that there is ugliness and horror too—is not to be minimized; and modern people are impoverished because they have let their imaginative perception atrophy. A reading of some of the poems of Gerard Manley Hopkins might help to restore this imaginative capacity; it is worth observing that in one poem Hopkins expressly equates beauty with the Holy Spirit who (as he says) "broods over the best world"—bent in that poem, not away from God, but toward him.

Yet it is true that the Holy Spirit is the Spirit of righteousness and goodness known in human history and in the affairs of people. God has his purpose for the world; that purpose is the establishment of an order in which goodness prevails and hence in which righteousness, the giving to all persons their proper due, must prevail also. Such an order in goodness and righteousness is a response to the good purpose, the good will, of God; and like all response, this is through the working of the Spirit. Thus part of the action of the Spirit in the world is the bringing of people into conformity with the intended pattern of goodness and righteousness. This is not necessarily an *obvious* action; we must again recall that the Holy Spirit often does his work anonymously. But where justice and peace, truth and understanding, human fellowship and cooperation are achieved, anywhere, anytime, by any group or individual, there the Holy Spirit is operative.

This operation presupposes human freedom of decision and human responsibility for the results of such decision. The decisions of people may be misguided, leading to distortion or deviation in human affairs. When that is the case, correction is required. At such points, the Spirit who normally works only in gentleness, persuasion, and mercy, may work in judgment. He must bend people's evil wills to God's good will, not by breaking people but by showing them the error and absurdity of setting themselves at the center of things and proudly pretending that they are "masters of all they survey." He must lead the people of the earth into obedience to God's will which is for their own best good, not by totally destroying them but by making plain to them the terrible results which follow upon selfish self-seeking, lust for power, attempts to dominate their fellowmen, and unjust treatment of helpless minorities. Such results will include the collapse of empires and nations, brought on themselves when they attempt to get along in supreme disregard of others or when they seek to control fellow human beings for their own ends. So it is that the Spirit speaks through the prophets, both ancient and modern; so it is that through him God raises up people who will put an end to oppression and wrong. This is the "terrible" aspect of the Spirit's working; but it is terrible only to those who are destroying themselves in the effort to destroy others. The prophets, inspired by the Holy Spirit, proclaim in no uncertain voice the truth which W. H. Auden spoke about in one of his poems when he said that we must love one another or die. The world is made like that; it is the Spirit who works to conform us to that world, both to our own greater good and by that very token to God's greater glory as the supremely loving and righteous One.

In simpler human relationships, including the love between people, the Holy Spirit is also at work. Ordinary human contacts, marked by friendliness and helpfulness, are not outside his range. Nowadays we hear much about "meeting," and some years ago Dr. J. H. Oldham coined the telling phrase, "all real life is meeting." But what is that meeting of person with person? It is mysterious in its personalizing capacity: it is the transformation of what might have been only the contact of two "its" into a sharing between an "I" and a "Thou." In the analysis of this "I-Thou" relationship by the Jewish scholar Martin Buber, we are told that whenever such a meeting occurs, there is always the hidden presence of "Another"; somehow it takes "three" to unite "two." Buber is saying in effect that God's Spirit is there, although as usual the Spirit is present in his anonymity. If that is true, as Buber's analysis shows, of ordinary human meetings, it is much more profoundly true in the most intimate relationship of person with person which we call love. There is good reason for the feeling that nobody can earn or merit the love of another; it is always "of grace," a gift which is given to each by the other and given to both by something in the nature of things in which they are enabled to participate. It is a work of the Spirit of God.

Above all for Christian faith, God's will for people is declared in Jesus Christ. In the full reality of manhood, lived out at a particular historical time and place (as human existence must always be), God's purpose is declared in terms that people can understand. Here most obviously the bringing of history into conformity with God's purpose, his declared will, is the work of the Holy Spirit. Here God's operation through the Holy Spirit is most certainly known on the level of conscious, personalizing action. Yet we need to remember that Jesus Christ is no alien intruder into the world; he is organic to it, from which in his manhood he emerged. His physical body, his psychological nature, indeed his total humanity are part of the ongoing process. A modern christology would also have to say that whatever is divine in that event is no alien intrusion either; it is a focusing and concentrating of what God is always doing in the creative advance. So it is also with the Holy Spirit. There is no absolute chasm between the activity of the Spirit in the natural order and that in the historical order, nor between the historical order and the human experience we all know, nor between that experience and the specific event of Jesus Christ. All is of one piece, although all is not of the same degree of intensity nor marked by the same qualitative impact.

Even in respect to Jesus, therefore, we cannot forget the levels of the divine activity below the properly personal, in the natural world and in physical and material things; the Spirit is also continuous in his operation through all these levels. The truth of this is illustrated plainly when we consider our own existence as persons. We live and work, we are or exist, not only on the level of conscious and personal action, but also on the level of subpersonal and unconscious life, with our physical functioning and with our chemical reactions and beneath them with our grounding in the subatomic creation. All these are as much a part of us as is our mental activity. Yet we tend to forget this and to think of ourselves as if we were "pure intelligences"—

72

the medieval definition of an angel. We are *not* angels; we are embodied persons. The Holy Spirit is operative on *all* those levels, so far as we are concerned; he is operative on all those levels in respect to his own "economy" in the world too. Economy is the theological term traditionally used to define the sort of activity which in the thinking of early theologians was appropriated to each hypostasis of the Godhead. Thus the economy of the Spirit is the conforming of the whole creation to the divine intention, so that that creation may properly respond to God and thereby achieve its perfection.

In other words, while the Holy Spirit is known to us who are on the way of becoming persons in terms of personalizing activity—and hence may rightly be regarded as truly personal in operation—he is also working on other and less than personalized and personalizing levels, including the natural order of things, the general range of historical action, and deep down in the unseen strata of our own human lives. To speak of him as the Spirit of the Christian church is to deny none of this. It is only to widen our vision of his pervasive and all-encompassing presence and power.

This wider vision has been put before us today in compelling terms in the writings of Pierre Teilhard de Chardin. He was a scientist who was also a Jesuit and a priest of the Roman Catholic Church. From his earliest days he was in love with the world of nature; there is the story of his sense of wonder when as a child he held a piece of rock in his hand and felt that in some strange fashion he and that rock belonged together. Throughout his life he saw the beauty and the strength of nature, but this did not for a moment reduce his faith in the God of nature. As he grew older he tried to put his vision into words. He wrote of the created order as providing us with a milieu which ultimately was divinely given; it was, indeed, the *divine milieu*. To be a person of faith did not require one to run away from the world, but to see God in and through the world. The world was a process in which with increasing complexity natural elements were making themselves—or so it might seem. But the truth was that the making of themselves was a making of them by God who was in them, drawing them on in their increasing complexity to serve ends which would give them satisfaction but which would also provide for God the instrument through which his "amorizing" work might be done. This work was indeed *truly* "amorizing," for it was an evocation of mutual relationships which in the end made possible the appearance of love (*amor*) such as human beings can know.

In that world Jesus Christ was born and lived. Teilhard said that the whole series of events which had preceded him had also prepared for him. Yet he was also a new appearance, not by contradicting or rejecting what had gone before but by disclosing the drive which had been present throughout the process. Now the creation has been opened up to respond to his influence as sheer love in act. *Christogenesis* had brought the possibility of "christification"—of "life in Christ," in Paul's phrase—both for people who respond to Christ and for the world as people see it relating to Christ. The goal of the process, which Teilhard called "the Omega point" when "Christ shall be all and in all," is a level of existence which in the New Testament is called the kingdom of God, where God declared in Christ as pure love would be fully known and served.

The details in Teilhard's writing have been criticized by scientists, philosophers, and theologians, but his overall vision is both noble and compelling. What is more, it is profoundly Christian. The tragedy is that the authorities of his own church did not recognize this and regarded him as dangerously speculative if not sometimes downright heretical. That is absurd. The one thing that we might wish to add to the Teilhardian picture is a stress on the place of the Holy Spirit in the creative process. However, this is implicit in his teachings and how we can see it has already been made clear in this chapter.

Teilhard was deeply Christian in his vision. Perhaps we may dare to claim that only a Christian could have had just that vision. For the Christian is the only one who knows the tremendous reality of God in the process of the world—for our present interest, the activity of God the Holy Spirit there. The Christian faith, finding its focus in Jesus Christ, can follow the rays there focused to their outermost point. To the Christian has been given the key to the secret. The Christian must recognize the universal, generous, persuasive, sometimes terrible action of God the Holy Spirit in the world of nature and of history, precisely because one has been given to know in one's heart and through one's sharing in the Christian fellowship the lure and the pressure of that Spirit. In loyal participation in the life of the Christian church the Christian knows togetherness in God, surrender to the divine will, and increasing growth in Christlikeness, which are all the work of "that one and the self-same Spirit." But one must *use* the key. One must see to it that one's own attitude toward the world reflects the desire to conform things to the divine purpose of love. One must labor to bring other people to share that desire that has taken possession of one's own life. Thus one is called to be a missionary in a sense much grander than the conventional one. For this mission is to invite his fellow humans to respond to God through the Spirit in the secular as well as in the religious areas of life. In particular one must help others to acknowledge that they too are caught up in the response which is the work of the Spirit. As one must live, so one must unfailingly act so that others may live, in the knowledge that "the Spirit of the Lord filleth the world." Then the day may come when all the earth will unite in making the answer to that Whitsuntide invitatory to the *Venite*: "O come, let us adore him. Alleluia."

6

The Spirit at Work in the Christian Fellowship

Now that we have seen the wider cosmic and historical context for the action of the Holy Spirit, it is safe (as we might put it) to stress the decisive quality of the working of the Spirit in the fellowship of Christian people to which we give the name church. The fellowship of Christians is so much the result of the Holy Spirit's action that it is appropriately called by Paul "the fellowship of the Holy Spirit" or "fellowship in Holy Spirit" or "fellowship through Holy Spirit," all three of which are possible ways of rendering his Greek words into English. They all come to the same thing, however. The Pauline letters and the whole of the New Testament resound with the note of joy and peace, love and sharing, which marked the lives of the early Christians as they found themselves bound together in a unity which was not of their own creation but was given to them.

There is every reason to think that there were misunderstandings, differences of opinion and practice, even quarrels, in the first days of the Christian community. Those who suppose that period entirely idyllic have not read the literature. Fallible people remained fallible; the ordinary human tendencies to willfulness were not abolished miraculously; people were still sinners, even if they knew within themselves the principle of redeemed life in Christ. But what strikes one in the New Testament and other very early Christian writing—such as the *Epistle to Diognetus*, the *Didache*, the letters from Clement of Rome, the letters of Ignatius—literature taking us to the turn of the first century and a little later—is the sense of an invigorating, unifying, utterly commanding reality which had taken possession of quite simple men and women and enabled them to give themselves as a company of Christians in complete dedication to Jesus Christ as their risen Lord. We might quote the familiar phrase of Robert Browning, from an entirely different context, and say that the peculiar characteristic of the earliest Christian community was its "first fine careless rapture." The last two words of that phrase are particularly apt, for there was a carelessness, an indifference to self and self-interest, and a rapturous enthusiasm and vitality, which no reader of the material can miss.

Earlier we mentioned Lionel Thornton's book *Common Life in the Body of Christ*. In that book and also in one chapter of his work *The Incarnate Lord*, he gives us what I believe remain the best descriptions in modern English theology of the atmosphere of those early days "in the Spirit." He shows how the remarkable variety of experience in the Christian community, as reflected for us in the New Testament, bears vivid witness to unity of spirit, a unity which the New Testament itself called "unity in the Spirit." It is extraordinary to observe how with all the diversity in approach, with the many different kinds of people drawn from many different backgrounds and cultures, and despite the patent contrast between those of the Jewish race and those of various Hellenistic or Graeco-Roman outlooks, a genuine and vital fellowship was established which spread through the eastern Mediterranean region and made converts everywhere.

We start as we must, from the simple facts of human experience in all their rich variety. We see the confidence, joy, and vitality, of a shared experience. We notice that this is related to what was for these people the absolutely basic reality—belief in, adoration of, and obedience to the risen Lord whose presence they felt and whose power they knew. As we look at these, we come to the point where we follow those early Christians in recognizing that the human facts are not readily explicable without the introduction of still another factor. We must move from the realm of the human into the realm where we can see God the Holy Spirit at work bearing witness with the human spirit and empowering people for their human response to the revelation of God in Christ.

The first point to stress is that this primitive Christian experience of the presence and power of the Holy Spirit was no purely individualistic matter but a social or corporate reality. A great enthusiasm bound the believers together into community. The commanding nature of this great enthusiasm made it seem entirely natural for them to say: "It seems good to the Holy Ghost *and to us*." Second, the vigor and refreshment induced by that enthusiastic response wrought remarkable changes in the lives of the men and women who were baptized into the fellowship of Christian faith. Even nonbelieving historians are obliged to comment on the changes. The great Gibbon, cynical enough about the Christian faith, could not omit a reference to the remarkable moral quality of the first Christians and was obliged to number this among the causes for the victory of the Christian church through persecution and suffering and over the older religious faiths of the Roman Empire.

We can see depressed people of the slave class and the riff-raff of the slums of the great cities, the licentious men and women of a place like Corinth—known throughout the Mediterranean as an immoral city, so much so that a verb *corinthizai* had been coined to describe the sexual laxity there—brought within the Christian churches in town after town. And having been accepted "just as they were," they began to show "fruits worthy of repentance." Again and again Paul mentions this in his letters. It must have astonished him to see people who at the time of their conversion to Christ had been lamentably weak, lustful, and degraded specimens of humanity, become men and women "in Christ." Yet his references to this change show that he well knew what had brought it about, for he himself had experienced just such a change. In his case, however, the change was not from licentiousness to purity but from narrowness of mind and refusal to move beyond the legalism of Jewish religion as often understood at the time, to the freedom and openness which he found in Christ, and found especially in membership in the Christian community in which eventually he became a leading figure.

Thus the fellowship of faith was quite properly called the fellowship of those who had "received" the Holy Spirit. For it was not a community brought into being by the Christians themselves, as if through their changed inner life as individual believers they had decided to come together in a society for its promotion in the world. Quite the contrary. It was not their creation, formed because by some happy chance they had hit upon certain important truths and found themselves agreeing on certain major beliefs and ideals. They were convinced that this fellowship had been *given to them*. They had been "called" to enter it. It had been established by God himself through his Spirit for them now to enter, and in it they were now enabled to share. We have just used the English word enthusiasm; it is appropriate, since it means "being in the divine," and this sense of "in-God-ness" (as we might phrase it) was the characteristic quality of the primitive Christian community. Here indeed was life "in Christ," through the Spirit, linking people in a strangely new way with "the love of God in Christ Jesus the Lord."

The early Christian theologian Irenaeus has some telling words in his book *Against Heresies*:

For God promised, that in the last times He would pour Him the Spirit upon His servants and handmaids, that they might prophesy; wherefore He did also descend upon the Son of God, made the Son of Man, becoming accustomed in fellowship with Him to dwell in the human race, to rest with human beings, and to dwell in the workmanship of God, working the will of the Father in them, and renewing them from their old habits into the newness of Christ.

This Spirit did David ask for the human race, saying "And stablish me with Thine all-governing Spirit"; who also, as Luke says, descended at the day of Pentecost upon the disciples after the Lord's ascension, having power to admit all nations to the entrance of life, and to the opening of the new covenant; from whence also, with one accord in all languages, they uttered praise to God, the Spirit bringing distant tribes to unity, and offering to the Father the first-fruits of all nations. Wherefore also the Lord promised to send the Com-

79

forter, who should join us to God. For as a compacted lump of dough cannot be formed of dry wheat without fluid matter, nor can a loaf possess unity, so, in like manner, neither could we, being many, be made one in Christ Jesus without the water from heaven [the reference, of course, is to the "gift of the Spirit" in Baptism and Confirmation which were inseparably one rite in Irenaeus' time]. And as dry earth does not bring forth unless it receives moisture, in like manner we also, being originally a dry tree, could never have brought forth fruit unto life without the voluntary rain from above. For our bodies have received unity among themselves by means of that washing which leads to incorruption; but our souls, by means of the Spirit . . . The Lord, receiving this [Spirit] as a gift from His Father, does Himself also confer it upon those who are partakers of Himself, sending the Holy Spirit upon all the earth.*

Even earlier, Ignatius of Antioch, writing to the Christians in Ephesus, said much the same when he spoke of being prepared for the building of God the Father, being raised up on high by Jesus Christ and his Cross, and *being drawn by the rope which is the Holy Spirit*, with faith as its pulley and love as the way leading to God.

But we need not continue with these quotations, which could be duplicated dozens of times from early Christian literature. The fact is plain: Here is a community united in every way to God the Father, in response to Jesus Christ, through the action of the Holy Spirit who moves in that community. Here, for those Christians, was a working of God, not something invented or created by their own effort. Yet on the other hand human effort *was* required. But it was *after* what Irenaeus called "entrance into life." The "fruit of the Spirit" was indeed a gift from that Spirit; and the working out in daily life of the fruit was the daily obedience of the Christian to the imperatives of love which were laid on him by the same Spirit.

We have said that in Christian thought it is correct to say that while the Holy Spirit is everywhere at work in the world and

* There are numerous translations of Irenaeus' *Against Heresies*. I am quoting from the edition printed in *The Ante-Nicene Fathers*, volume I, edited by Alexander Roberts and James Donaldson (New York: Charles Scribner's Sons, 1899), Book III, Chapter XVII, pp. 444-45.

hence everywhere to be recognized and adored wherever he is seen, he is supremely, decisively, and one might almost say "visibly" at work in the Christian fellowship. Thus the church, which the New Testament calls the Body of Christ, is the place where the Holy Spirit is *intensively* present and *intensively* active.

Everything rightly done in the church is done in the power of the Holy Spirit. When this truth is forgotten—and alas, it has often been forgotten by ecclesiastical dignitaries as well as by ordinary believers—the church deteriorates into a dull and dead mechanism. It concerns itself only with its own "domestic housekeeping," spending its time in revising its canons, in reordering its financial affairs, in preserving its buildings, and in all those other affairs which make many outsiders think that it is at best a museum piece and at worst a useless bit of society's organizational structure with no purpose save making its own wheels go round. Failure to discern the Spirit and to obey his voice means that the church's existence becomes static, not dynamic; it turns what ought to be a thrilling and exciting movement toward augmenting love among people into a conventional institution where all too often the *odium theologicum* prevails. When, on the other hand, the Holy Spirit is recognized and welcomed into his due place of authority and of control, the life of the church flowers into a wonderful richness and the church moves through the world "as an army with banners."

Indeed, even when the Spirit is not recognized and his presence forgotten, he is not absent from the church. He works there hiddenly and secretly; and sooner or later, as history demonstrates, he effects a revival or reformation in the institution. In the Middle Ages this happened with Francis of Assisi and his band of friars. The Reformation revitalized the community, even if it caused schism. More recently in the Church of England the Wesleyan movement had the same result. In our own time ecumenical interest, liturgical awakening, astounding concern shown for social problems, racial integration, and the like, may be taken as still another illustration of this process by which the Spirit reanimates what seems to be a nearly dead body. With all its eccentricities and excesses, it may very well be the case that the Pentecostal movement now appearing in North America and elsewhere is especially an arousal by the Spirit of a new enthusiasm and vigor in Christian institutional life.

After all, there can be no genuine Christianity without fellowship; the church, in that sense, is part of the gospel itself. In the New Testament, to be a Christian *means* to belong to the new Israel of God. The notion that anybody can be a Christian, save in the most attenuated sense (apart from what Baron Von Hügel quaintly called "church appurtenance") is a comparatively modern and in scriptural terms an entirely fallacious, notion. Hence we may conclude that the very fact of Christian fellowship demonstrates that the Holy Spirit is always there in the church, although he is not always given due acknowledgment and permitted to play his role. But "the wind bloweth where it listeth"; so the Spirit moves where and as he will. He can make "even these dead bones to live," as the Old Testament writer saw in respect to Israel; and he has done just that again and again in the Christian community throughout its long and sometimes distressing history.

The church is the closely knit, interpenetrative, and organically integrated vehicle by which Jesus Christ our Lord continues uniquely to accomplish his purposes in the world. That is what is meant by calling it "the Body of Christ"—it is Christ's special way, although by no means his only way, of "getting himself across," of "expressing himself," in the world of people and history. The Lord Christ is the "Head of the Body," and the Holy Spirit is rightly interpreted as the informing and conforming life of the Body. It is he who binds it together in the unity of response to Christ to which we have referred so often—the nature of his work, the intention with which he works, and the results which follow from his work, are all defined for us by Christ. Here is the difference between the working of the Spirit outside the empirical church, in every part of the world, and the working of the Spirit within the church.

Recognizing this genuine distinction, some theologians have presumed to argue that there are, so to say, two "spirits." But this will not do since God's work in creaturely response is all of a piece; it is of the same quality everywhere. He is the God of order, not of confusion. It is indeed difficult always to hold together a both-and; it is so much easier to speak of an either-or.

It requires effort to maintain universality and uniqueness, the pervasive and the particular, the general and the special in our thinking, without making a false dichotomy between the terms in each of those distinctions. But the Christian theologian and the Christian disciple too, in his less articulate way, must do just this, above all with the Spirit's working in church and world.

There is an important corollary to our belief in the church as the Body of Christ. Paul Tillich used to point this out, although what he said could be paralleled largely from other and earlier writers. Tillich made a distinction between what he styled the church as a "latent" reality, in that the potentiality of "church-ness" is found in all those areas where the Spirit is at work in response to Christ, and the church as "manifestation," where there is a conscious awareness of this response. This suggests to us that we must not try to define too closely what is intended when we say that the Spirit works in the church. We should be wary, indeed distrustful, of those definitions which are supposed to tell us with neat precision just who is and just who is not "of the church." That is for God to decide, not for us. Yet this does not involve any woolly idea of the nature of the church. We can be as clear as we wish about what are the central and necessary "notes" in the church's existence—and to these we shall turn immediately—without succumbing to the temptation to delimit the churchly working of the Holy Spirit and to dictate to Christ just where he shall and where he shall not be disclosed to awaken that Spirit's response.

Traditionally four "notes" of the church have been given: unity, holiness, apostolicity, and catholicity. We repeat those words when in the Nicene Creed we affirm our belief: "We believe in one Holy Catholic and Apostolic Church." Let us look at these traditional notes and see how they fit into the developing pattern of this discussion of the Holy Spirit at work in the Body of Christ.

The church, we say, is *one*. But it is not one because all Christians are at this moment empirically united in an outwardly visible institution. It is one because the Holy Spirit works in and through all who profess and call themselves Christian to conform them to the one Lord "in the unity of the Spirit, in the bond of peace, and in righteousness of life." They make their response together and as one, although not always visibly, to that Lord.

The church, we say, is *holy*. But its holiness is not because the members of the church individually, nor for that matter the church as an observable society always and everywhere, appear to manifest moral holiness. The church is holy because the Holy Spirit works in and through the community of Christian believers both to set them "apart from the world"—in that they are not to give their final allegiance to created things or mortal goods— and to send them on a mission to the world, bringing the life of Christ to men and women everywhere.

The church, we say, is *catholic*. But its catholicity does not consist in some institutional pattern however ancient and hallowed, nor even in the fact that it is "universally known and universally extended," as some of the older theological textbooks used to say. But it is catholic because it is *whole*, integrated by the Spirit and the response in the Spirit into an organism (*kath olou* is the Greek phrase behind catholic and its meaning is "in terms of wholeness") in Christ and thus *made* whole through the Spirit whose presence and power make for just this wholeness and integration.

We say that the church is *apostolic*. It is apostolic, not through the structures which link it to its formative period, upon which an older theology insisted with an almost demonic intensity; but through the working of the Spirit within it who sends it out into the world and enables it to remember always that first sending in the apostolic age. It is thus linked to the response of those who first knew the Lord Christ, who companied with him, and who handed down the story of his impact upon them.

If we interpret the notes of the church in this way, so also we must interpret every action of the church in its worship and in its witness. Here again what is performed is done in the power of the Holy Spirit. The gospel of God in Christ is proclaimed, as we often say, "in his power." The eucharist is celebrated in the Spirit-filled community by those who are strengthened in the Spirit and obedient to his will. Christian life, both in the interior sense of communion with God and in the external sense of behavior among people, is life in the Spirit; and it manifests, if the Spirit is allowed to have his way, those fruits to which Paul

84

and the rest of the New Testament bear witness. Therefore, in all its discipleship to Christ, the church is made into the fellowship in which the Holy Spirit is indeed working distinctively. When it *is* this, it realizes and fulfills its function as the Body of Christ.

The channels through which the life of the Christian in the church is empowered are the sacraments: baptism by which we become "very members incorporate in the mystical Body of Christ" and Holy Communion in which we partake of the risen life of Christ. The other rites and ceremonies observed in one way or another by many Christians. such as marriage, confirmation, absolution or forgiveness of sin declared by an accredited minister of the church, anointing of the sick and dying, and holy orders, have been called further "means of grace," through which strengthening is made available to God's children within the church. But we do not always remember that the effectiveness of *all* these, not only of the eucharist, is dependent upon the Holy Spirit's action. Perhaps this becomes most clear to us in baptism and the rite of confirmation, which is the completion of baptism but which is unhappily separated from its "parent" rite in the Western, although not in the Eastern church. All these ecclesiastical activities are in danger of becoming *mere* rites and ceremonies unless the Spirit "enables" them, making them significant, dynamic, and life-giving ordinances. Were it not for the Spirit in the Body, the church's sacramental actions might seem to descend to an almost magical level; because they are Spirit-empowered they are genuinely religious actions. For religion is a conforming of people to God and his all-perfect will, while magic is an attempt to twist God's purpose to serve purely human ends. More must be said about the Holy Spirit in Christian worship in the next chapter. It is a subject whose importance is far too often neglected in theological discussion.

We have repeatedly stressed the unity of Christians through the fellowship of the Holy Spirit. This must now be given a little more attention, if for no other reason than that it helps to explain how in the Christian church throughout the world, even in times so terrible as World War II, the church was held together by bonds which were so strong that none of the usual divisive elements in human experience could pull it to pieces.

85

In the early days of the church, as reflected in the Acts of the Apostles, there was unity in the Spirit despite serious disagreements. These disagreements included whether or not the old Jewish dietary laws were to be observed, whether circumcision was to be required of every convert who was not a Jew, and whether in general the Jewish Torah was to be as much obligatory on members of the "new Israel" as it had been on members of the "old." Paul was not talking fancifully when he said that "in Christ"—which, as we have noted, meant for him as for all first-century Christians to be in the church which was Christ's Body —there is neither Jew nor Greek, circumcised nor uncircumcised, barbarian, Scythian, bondman nor freeman. Neither was there any distinction in that membership between "male and female." *All* who responded to Christ were one in Christ through the Spirit. That was the great new fact which so vividly struck the outside world. Not too much later Tertullian, the North African lawyer-convert to Christianity, could point out how pagans were obliged to say, "See how these Christians love one another!" He did not intend that report to be ironical either, as we might think it today; it was simply the truth. Those who thus "loved one another" were of every type and race and class; the "love of God in Christ Jesus," shed abroad through the Spirit of God, made it a plain fact to be seen by the outsider. The things which usually separate people from one another, such as racial background and color, culture or economic position, or sex, were overcome in the strength of a unity which held them together in a common faith, a common love, and a common purpose. Of that unity the common meal, the eucharist, was the outward and visible sign and also the empowering action. In all these ways men and women, without regard for who they were or what they were or where they were, were made one in the Spirit. It was the Spirit who had brought them into discipleship to Christ in the church and who day by day conformed them to him who was the pattern of true humanity in true community.

Thus we return to our insistence that the work of the Holy Spirit within the fellowship of Christians is primarily to conform people to Jesus Christ. This is the deepest truth about the Spirit in the church's corporate experience, for the conforming

86

is inevitably a social fact and not a purely individualistic one. The reason is apparent: The church is the Body of Christ in which all members are one with their Head; or in the Johannine image, he is the Vine of which the branches are part. The church is not a congeries of individual men and women who happen to think the same way and do the same things; it is a corporate reality, not merely a collection of individual men and women.

We have stressed the significance of the "Pentecostal revival" in our time. We may agree with Lesslie Newbigin's comment in *The Household of God* that while for a long time we recognized in one way or another the catholic or structural element in the Christian church and the reforming and corrective evangelical element, we did not sufficiently recognize the "pentecostal" element. The "holiness sects," with all their strangeness, have something to say to us. It is not in their shouting or in their claims to manifest "peculiar gifts of the Spirit" that they can teach us. Rather, it is in their insistence that the church is the community in which men and women are caught up by and strengthened in the Spirit of God. How this may manifest itself is a different matter. Perhaps relatively few people are likely to be exuberant in the way found in those sects, although Dr. Haroutunian has rightly noted that "the work of the Spirit in the Church" may very well entail "ecstacy and ecstacy will not be contained by convention."* Those who know the Spirit may very well find themselves moved from time to time "to extraordinary and unexpected behaviour." A friend once remarked, after attending a very staid and respectable churchservice in the chapel of the theological college where I taught, "What would happen if some of those students and professors really 'got religion' and began to show it in their actions right there in chapel?" One does not know what would have happened; in any event, it was wrong of my friend to assume that the following of a liturgical form of worship cannot be accompanied by genuine enthusiasm which does not show itself in obvious ways.

* Joseph Haroutunian, "Spirit, Holy Spirit, Spiritism," *A Dictionary of Christian Theology*, ed. Alan Richardson (London: SCM Press, Ltd., 1969), p. 327.

But it *might* show itself that way sometimes—and if it did, those who were present would perhaps be the better for it!

Finally, we need to remember that to be conformed to Christ through the Spirit may not only be manifested in spiritual enthusiasm and even excitement; it may also mean sacrifice and suffering. Nowadays that thought does not much appeal to ordinary church people, although in some parts of the world such sacrifice and suffering is the norm for Christian disciples. We who live in countries where there is no persecution of the church (at least, in any obvious way) often tend to think of sacrifice in a rather muted sense: It is doing without chocolates in Lent or saving a little money for the purpose of making a donation to a good cause. One need not denigrate such "sacrifices" when one says that Christian sacrifice is altogether more demanding than that.

In the relatively affluent Western world, we generally think of Christian faith and of participation in the church's life as if it were entirely a matter of helping us to live whole, full, abundant lives. That is part of the truth but not all of it. There is another side. Whole, full, abundant lives can only be had if the gospel of the cross is true, through radical transformation. Jesus himself told us that sometimes an evil eye must be plucked out, a diseased limb cut off, drastic measures taken if we are to secure true health for the "whole body." And while he himself was entirely given to the service of his heavenly Father, yet he "learned obedience by the things that he suffered." The Holy Spirit in the church is the Spirit who moves us to discipline our lives. This discipline is of mind and body. It is called in Greek *ascesis*, which means "athletic life." There is a place for that *ascesis* in the discipleship of every Christian, and the church is where one may learn this truth. So the fellowship of the Spirit is also "the fellowship of Christ's sufferings," as the New Testament tells us. *Ascesis* is an obligation that is laid in some sense and with some degree of demand upon every member of the church, in every vocation and ministry.

Thus sacrificial participation in the Christian community *is* Christian existence, and it is "of the Spirit." But there is more to be said. For to be complete, what is being worked out in and through us must be expressed in all human relationships, in

88

daily life and in common duties, in the life of society and in the work of the world. The grace of God, given by the Holy Spirit, comes to Christians as a gift which is also their task. That is inescapable. To be a Christian is to be one of the channels through which the life of Christ known in the Spirit's fellowship pours out into the life of the world.

So the church is essentially a missionary society. It is called to share the gifts which it has received. As a corporate entity and through its particular members, it is to exhibit the love, joy, peace, long-suffering, meekness, temperance, which are the "fruit of the Spirit." Perhaps in our own day it is called especially to witness to and to work for justice among people in social affairs, in racial relations, and in the achievement of peace among the peoples and nations of the earth. In all these ways it is to bring all people, in the Spirit, to Christ, and through Christ to the Father, that "God may be all and in all."

This is "in the meantime," between the first coming of Christ and the day in which God's will is done "in earth as it is in heaven," pictured for us symbolically as the "second coming of Christ." In this "meantime," Christians are not left without a Comforter, an Advocate, an Inspirer. The Holy Spirit has been "shed abroad" in their hearts, not for the first time but with singular intensity and directness. The church has been created, where life in Christ through the Spirit may be shared. We live, indeed, "in hope"; but we live *by* faith and *with* love—which is to say that we live in the Spirit of Christ who is the Spirit of God. The communion which Christians have one with another in the Body of Christ nourishes them in the faith, strengthens them in the love, and encourages them in the hope which is the strong expectation of "the glory which shall be revealed in 'the last day.'" Life "in the meanwhile" is therefore a joyous life, as Christian life, truly lived, must always be.

By the Spirit, known in the church of Christ, Christian men and women have the assurance that he in whom they have believed is steadfast; they can be "persuaded that he is able to keep all that they have committed to him, until 'That Day'"— the day when, as the words of the Advent collect put it in high symbolism but with telling effect, "he shall come again in his glorious majesty, to judge both the quick and the dead."

7

The Spirit at Work in Worship

The Christian tradition as we have inherited it and as we live in it is like a cord composed of three strands. Each of those strands is essential to the whole cord; each of them is strengthened by the other strands. Any one of them taken alone is inadequate to the rich and complex organic wholeness of Christianity, and taken by itself cannot be properly understood and interpreted.

The first of these strands is the Christian *faith*, in which through commitment to the activity of God in Jesus Christ (which in scholastic terms is the *fides qua fidetur*, the faith by which one believes) the Christian is led to an ever more profound understanding of God, his nature, his activity, his purpose, and his relationship with the world. That understanding, in the same scholastic idiom, is *fides quae creditur*—the faith which one believes. The second strand is *worship*: how God is to be adored in the light of that which in Jesus Christ he has accomplished "for us men and for our salvation." The third strand comprises *discipleship*: the workaday life of the Christian and the internal spirit which enables and illuminates that life. This strand is what the Christian is and does because one believes in and worships God in Christ.

In the course of our study we have said much about Christian faith, as this relates especially to the Holy Spirit. In the chapter which follows this one, we shall have much to say about the living out of that faith in the power of the Holy Spirit. In the present chapter we are particularly interested in the worship of the Christian community which, as we have already insisted, is "in the power" of the same Holy Spirit. The logic ought to be plain. First there must be commitment to God, known in Christ, to make us Christian. Then there must be a relationship to God, through the church's acts of adoration and praise. Finally, these two will lead, or ought to lead, to the inner relationship with God that will produce outward acts that reflect God's nature as shared with his children.

It is true, of course, that this logic is not always followed in the concrete experience of a Christian. Very often it is through one's participation in the church's worship that one comes to grasp something of the faith and is prepared to make the act of surrender or commitment to God in Christ. Sometimes it is by "doing the works" of Christ that one finds oneself drawn to worship and commitment. Nobody should insist that each Christian must of necessity follow the proper logic of the Christian tradition's historical development in theological understanding. Yet that logic does make sense and ought not to be entirely disregarded. This is especially true in such a study as we are undertaking, where our effort is to show the way in which the Christian's existence with other persons in the community of the Spirit works itself out in specific ways.

It is appropriate to speak of the Spirit at work in Christian worship. It has always been maintained in the tradition that worship is not only the central aspect of a sound Christian life, but that the significance of this worship is never found simply and solely in human concern but is by and in and of the Holy Spirit. Thomas Aquinas wrote that all genuinely Christian worship is offered *to* God as Father, *through* the mediation of God the Son who in Christ is incarnate to make God known to us and bring us to him, and *in* the Holy Spirit, who "takes of the things of Christ" and who informs the members of the Body of Christ so that they are made free and willing instruments in giving God the glory which is his due.

91

This is true of *all* worship within the Christian church. It is supremely true of liturgical worship, which finds its culmination and focus in the eucharistic action which we call the Holy Communion, the Great Thanksgiving, the Lord's Supper, the Divine Mysteries, or the Mass—depending upon the idiom of the particular group of present-day Christians. But worship in *all* its expressions is the common task of the church as it offers itself and those who are its members to God. And worship is varied in type.

The *Opus Dei* (the "work of God") is the name which has been given to the "daily office" in traditional Christian circles. For Anglicans and Lutherans this is Morning and Evening Prayer which (as the English Prayer Book remarks) are to be read "daily throughout the year." In other Christian bodies, less liturgical in their tradition, there are services of worship which are similar in intention to the *Opus Dei*, even if they are not performed every day of the week but only on the Lord's Day or Sunday. The *Opus Dei* leads to the central liturgical act of the church in the Holy Eucharist. Here the family of God in a given place gathers round the family table to make its "offering of praise" to the Father and to receive from God's hand the nourishment or food which is the risen life of Jesus Christ himself as he makes himself available to the faithful communicant. Our attention naturally will be given particularly to that act of worship, precisely because of its centrality. Someone has remarked that if a man from Mars came to earth, the best way to acquaint him with the thing we call Christianity would be to take him to some place where the eucharist is being offered. He would learn much more about the reality of Christianity there than if we read him bits of the Bible or repeated the words of the creed. For the Christian church is "at work in worship," and as we shall see, this means that the *Holy Spirit* is at work in worship.

The ancient Christian theologian Irenaeus has this to say in the work *Against Heresies* from which we have already quoted:

God after his great goodness poured his compassion upon us, through which compassion "the Dayspring from on high hath looked upon us, and appeared to those who sat in darkness and the shadow of death, and has guided our feet into the way of peace...." For all things had entered upon a new phrase, when the Word arranged after a new manner his advent in the flesh, that he might win us back to God in the human nature which had departed from God. *Therefore men were taught to worship God after a new fashion.**

We may not like the phrase about man's nature "departing from God," although if we understand this to mean that people have failed to follow the direction which God wills in the creative advance of the process we may well accept what Irenaeus says. But we cannot doubt that he is speaking the truth when he tells us that "men were taught to worship God after a new fashion." For while the Christian eucharist has its Jewish background and parallels and can only be given its proper theological significance in the light of Jewish worship, it is also obvious that the eucharist *is* "a new fashion" in worship—it is a participation in "the new and living way" to God the Father which in Jesus Christ is offered to God's children. Even if we also grant, as we must, that in the eucharist there are certain parallels to ideas and practices found in the "mystery cults" of the Graeco-Roman world in the first centuries of our era, and indeed some parallels to sacred sacramental meals elsewhere in the world, the *novelty* of Christian eucharistic worship is apparent. Those parallels and resemblances in fact are not merely the discovery of recent scholarship, at least in respect to the Jewish background. Thomas Aquinas in one of his eucharistic hymns explicitly states that the eucharist is "the newer rite" which fulfills (and hence brings to their end, both as fulfillment and as termination) earlier "types and shadows." It is natural, one can even say inevitable, that non-Christian worship, wherever it is found, shall be in some way a preparation for Christian worship. The human is human, no matter where one may live or in what age one may worship; and one's yearning for a way of worshiping God, which shall both please God and fulfill human life, is all of a piece.

Thus we can say that the Holy Spirit not only has "taken of the things of Christ" and made their meaning plain, he has also taken of the natural human desire to be in contact with

* Irenaeus, *Against Heresies*, op. cit., 444-45.

God and to worship him, and he has filled these things with the meaning given all life by Christ. As Dr. Percy Gardner once put it, by the Spirit every good thing in the world is "baptized into Christ." Even those things which are imperfect and defective receive their correction by the Spirit and thus are susceptible to use by that same Spirit for the accomplishment of the purposes of God declared in Christ. To say this is in no sense to succumb to easy toleration or complacency. It is only to recognize that God has never left himself "without witness" in men's hearts and that the working of the Spirit can and does purify as well as confirm everything in the creation which, according to God's intention, is a *good* creation through which he ceaselessly and faithfully acts *for* good. Tennyson had something of this vision when in the familiar words about prayer found in *Idylls of the King* he wrote that the round world is in every way bound by gold chains about the feet of God.

It is tragic that more Christians have not been prepared to see this and act upon it when they contemplate what to them appear primitive or even barbaric rites and ceremonies. Instead of simple denunciation, it would be better to acknowledge them as people's groping attempt to be in communion with the one and only God—an attempt which is a response, however distorted, to a genuine activity of God in them and upon their lives.

The eucharistic action is a "remembering" of the life, death, resurrection, and ascension of Jesus Christ. It is the characteristic action of the Christian church because in dramatic terms it placards before the world, and offers in the "presence of the divine majesty," the significance of Christ's act. Thus it "comprehends the whole mystery of our redemption," as Thomas Aquinas put it. Here there is enacted before us, in that which Christ "commanded us to do in his remembrance," the faith which lives at the heart of the Christian fellowship. This is the church's offering of itself, because the church which is Christ's Body offers itself to God *as* his Body and receives back from him its own life, strengthened by the sacramental Body of Christ for its work in the world. Augustine could tell his hearers that "the mystery of themselves is on the altar"; Aquinas could say that the *res* (the innermost reality) of the sacrament is the unity of the Christian church. And in our own day Dom Gregory Dix could tell us that by this eucharistic action the church is continually being made into that which it is: Christ's Body corporate through participation in Christ's sacramental body.

We can speak of "the power of the Holy Spirit" because the Spirit is ultimately at work in the church's supreme worship. He makes possible the offering to God the Father of "the continual remembrance of the sacrifice of the death of Christ." No man could venture to approach God in so intimate and direct a fashion as the Holy Communion, were it not for that empowering by the Spirit. Above all, no man would "make bold to say," in the most personal and confident terms, that God is "Father"—as Christians dare in the eucharistic repetition of the Lord's Prayer —if God himself in the person of the incarnate Son had not "taught us to say" it by word and deed, and if the Spirit did not make it possible for people to come immediately and without fear into the field of power where God energizes so directly in human life. "No man can see God and live," the Old Testament says; that is true enough, in its way. Yet by the Holy Spirit people can come to the "mercy-seat" without cringing in fear but with reverent awe of him who is the Holy One, "dwelling in light unapproachable and full of glory."

Joining with Christian brethren in this privilege of worship through the eucharist, we know that such worship has reality and significant meaning only by and in the Holy Spirit, in the church, in the fellowship which has bound us into a unity which nothing in this world can break. His is the fellowship of the church; his is the enabling of the response of people to God made manifest; his is the gift of adoration and of thankful reception of the "life which is life indeed." Yet this is without in any way abrogating or denying the full freedom of human participation. To think that the Holy Spirit overrode or negated that freedom, with its decisions made by each person for oneself, would be seriously to confuse matters. The Spirit works in and through human freedom, not against it; his action is in making it possible for us freely to choose that which is for our own good rather than to be imprisoned in the choice of what is against that best good. Thus in the eucharist, our free human act in doing what Christ commanded is inspired but not coerced by the Spirit's invitation and solicitation.

It is hardly necessary to remark what an enormous difference such an awareness of human freedom and the Spirit's working can make in our ordinary experience of worship. To realize this double truth is to be delivered from all thought of triviality, cheapness, superficiality, irreverence, and (perhaps most important) boredom or tedium. Worship is then undertaken in the realization that it is worship "in the Spirit and in truth." "In the Spirit" because it is he who is at work to enable us to worship; "in truth" because it is utterly *real*, a matter of real things done by real people with a real purpose. Failure at this point is the explanation of the dullness and drabness so many find in the church's services. It is a terrible judgment upon the institutional church and its members that they have lost this vision so often and so thoughtlessly. We have been playing with dynamite—the *dynamis* or power of God the Spirit—as if we were toying with children's dolls. We have forgotten that the divine energy is to be released in this act of Christian worship; we have entered lightly and carelessly upon what is literally the most tremendous thing in the world. Hence we have been, and many of us still are, unprofitable servants of the Lord whom we claim to worship and in whose service we claim to be engaged. Irenaeus had a word to give us about what the church in its worship should look like. He spoke of the Body of Christ as pure and resplendent, being adorned within by the Word, and shielded on the outside by the Spirit, in order that from both, the splendor of Christ's natures as divine and human might be exhibited together. One can only admit in shame that all too frequently nothing of the sort is visible to the outsider and little of it is appreciated by church people.

There is still another implication of the fact that God the Holy Spirit is at work in worship. The whole world is the sphere in which he is moving to conform all things to their Creator's purpose declared in Christ, to bring them to God and to the accomplishment of his will for them. So, in our worship, it is not the worshiper alone, it is not even the "remembrance" of Jesus Christ alone, that is thankfully offered to God by the power of the Holy Spirit. The whole world and every bit of that world are offered. We offer our daily work, our jobs, our homes, our friendships, our loves, our tools and our possessions, our achievements, the social life which is ours, our relationships with others, even our failures. In fact, everything that we have and everything that we are, together with the whole world, are offered to God when we say that "with angels and archangels, and with all the company of heaven, we laud and magnify thy holy name; evermore praising thee, and saying, Holy, Holy, Holy, Lord God of hosts, heaven and earth are full of thy glory: Glory be to thee, O Lord most high . . ." In the old Anglican prayer of "oblation" the same thing is said: "And although we be unworthy, through our manifold sins, to offer unto thee any sacrifice; yet we beseech thee to accept this our bounden duty and service; not weighing our merits, but pardoning our offenses, through Jesus Christ our Lord . . ." followed by the great doxology: "by whom, and with whom, in the unity of the Holy Ghost, all honor and glory be unto thee, O Father almighty, world without end . . ." *That* is what the Holy Spirit at work in our worship makes possible for us.

Because God the Holy Spirit is at work with us in our worship, he provides us with a new perspective. At work *in* our worship, he works *through* our worship. He offers our praises to God on our behalf; and he sends us forth from worship with a new and refreshing insight into the nature of things as they really are in God's sight, with an understanding which can well be phrased in American idiom: he shows us "how things really stack up." In the liturgical worship of the Christian fellowship, we are enabled to see what comes first in life; our priorities are correctly ordered. Having enabled us to grasp this proper ordering, he sends us into the world to put those first things first and other things in their rightful places.

More and more we Christians have been forced to admit, after two devastating wars and the revelation of the limits to which people can go in selfishness and distortion of the good, that this world as it is can never become the kingdom of God in its fullness. At the same time, our realism in this respect is qualified by an even deeper realism: the realism of God himself. If this world is not the kingdom of God, as it stands here and now and if more education, more privileges, more satisfactory arrangement of its affairs will not "bring in that kingdom" or even its secular substitute "utopia"—although this is true, yet the Holy

Spirit working through our experience of worship of God makes us see that the world can come a great deal closer than we may commonly be ready to allow to the state of affairs in which love is regnant, and the kingdom of God is a fact. Furthermore, while no effort of people can "bring in" the kingdom, since it is God's to give and not ours to build, the Holy Spirit enables us to realize that we have both the responsibility and the opportunity to "prepare and make ready the way" for that kingdom which God in his good pleasure will bring. The vivid language we have just used is drawn from the *Book of Common Prayer*. It is a way of saying that although God's kingdom is really *himself*, as he takes into his own life and uses for good whatever is accomplished in creation, yet we are in duty bound to do our utmost, to strain every effort, for the bringing of the various spheres of our secular existence in this world "into obedience to Christ" and hence into conformity with the divine purpose of love which moves through all things in their creative advance. When worship fails to bring us this sense of responsibility, it has not been worship "in the Spirit and in truth," for we have then refused to permit the Holy Spirit to work upon us through the worship which he inspires. Then what we have been doing is a sham and a fraud. And thus, as we shall see in the following chapter, worship which is in the Spirit naturally, indeed inevitably, leads to Christian life in action in the world because it has done something radically new to our personal lives.

All this tells us that worship cannot become a private cult for our own delight. Indeed we dare not call that kind of worship genuinely Christian. Here we touch on a point that is of enormous importance today, since for many good and devout church people worship has become the enjoyment of a precious personal intimacy with God. The "early morning service," with very few present, is a symbol of what is wrong with such notions. One does not wish to deride anything that has been helpful to Christians at any time, yet the idea that "early service" in a dark church with a half-dozen other Christians, where the believer has a private tête-à-tête with God, is a travesty of genuine Christian worship. That sort of thing is slowly dying out, and for this we may be duly grateful. More and more Christians are coming to see that a *family* service, where "family" means the

98

family of Christ in a given place, is the norm of worship. Yet there are more than enough people who prefer the other way. With all their obvious goodness and piety, one can only say that these people need to be "converted." By this I mean that they need to "change their minds" and to be "turned round," so that they will come to understand the social reality of Christian discipleship. And here the Spirit is indeed teaching us all that true worship is the public work of the whole church.

Since it is this, it is for all people. The church itself is meant by God to include men and women of every type: black, white, yellow; German, Italian, Japanese, Russian, as well as English and American; rich, poor, simple, wise. The church, said Augustine, is a *corpus permixtum*. An old teacher of mine was accustomed to translating that Latin phrase as a "mixed bag." What is true of the church in God's intention is true also of worship as the church's public work. It is universal in its sweep and intended to be available for all people. This is why supreme blasphemy is seen in those parts of the world where black and white people are not permitted by law to worship in the same place at the same time.

Not long ago a friend told me that he had been talking with a regular churchgoer in the southern United States. In the course of the conversation, this layman touched on the question of racial segregation in worship and his own attitude toward it. He said, "Damn it, parson, I just hate to have those niggers around." Then he stopped himself and said, "Excuse me, parson, I didn't mean to be blasphemous." "How blasphemous?" said my friend. "Saying 'damn' in the presence of a clergyman," was the reply. "Oh," answered my friend, "you *were* blasphemous, but it wasn't in saying 'damn'; it was in saying that you hated having those niggers around." This attitude, this desire to have men and women of another race forbidden access to worship when Whites are engaging in what they take to be worship, is evidence that what they "take to be worship" is not worship at all, in the Spirit of God. It is a blasphemous sham, a denial of the faith they profess, and a shutting of the doors of their own hearts to the Spirit of God.

When a bishop once said that "the Church's task is to build more altars in more places," he was of course partially right. But the full truth is that there must first be more places where the way has been "prepared and made ready," so that the altars to be built will be *true* altars, where God is truly worshiped in the Spirit who conforms people to Christ. Otherwise, whatever is built will be but a table for idols or a sanctuary in which selfishness, pride, arrogance, bitterness, injustice, and all unloveliness will be cultivated. To fail to see this is to announce that we have failed to understand Christianity and that we do not know where the Spirit leads us as we seek to adore the one true God.

As we end this chapter, something should be said that may possibly lead to misunderstanding and may also seem to contradict much of what was urged in the last few paragraphs. There is a profound sense in which worship *is* the purpose for which everything else exists. The Westminster Catechism puts this in a superb sentence: "Man's chief end is to glorify God and to enjoy him forever." To glorify God is to give God the adoration and praise which is his due, precisely because he *is* the altogether adorable and the one who is to be praised. To enjoy him forever is to find in his presence true and abundant happiness. Both these are made available to his human children as they engage in the act of worship.

People do not worship God in order that they may work effectively in the world. They do not "come to church" in order to be made better men and women. The order of things should be reversed. In consequence of our worship of God we are enabled to work more effectively in the world, to be sure; as a result of "coming to church" we may very well become better men and women. Yet the *right* ordering is just the opposite. Here is the part that may be misunderstood. We work better so that we may worship God aright; we try to make the world a fit place for all human beings so that we and they may adore God as he should be adored; and we strive to be better, through the grace given us, so that we may fitly enter into "his gates with thanksgiving and into his courts with praise." In other words, the Christian's task is to labor to make the created order in its every corner a sanctuary where with all of their lives and in all of their works people worship God at every moment of their existence. The reality of worship is determined by the kind of work we do day by day.

I have said that this may be misunderstood. It is often assumed that we *earn* the right to worship—a view that is a sort of modernized Pelagianism, in which good works are the price we pay for the privilege of God's grace. My contention is entirely different. Nobody ever *earns* God's grace or the right to worship; the doctrine of justification by grace through faith is the cornerstone of all Christian life and the clue to all Christian thinking. What I am here urging is that *because* we have been "justified" —in Paul Tillich's striking phrase, because "we have been accepted by God even though we are unacceptable"—we are put in the way of serving God in the affairs of daily life. We *must* so serve him; then we shall be able to bring everything we are and have done to the altar of God, recognizing fully the imperfection in all that has been done and the imperfection in ourselves. At the altar we dare to offer "ourselves, our souls and bodies," together with our work *and* our failures of which we now repent, to God "as a reasonable, holy, and living sacrifice."

The practical moral here is that the witness of our lives must itself be an invitation to others to join us in the worship of God. That is part of the missionary task of Christian people: to bring to all people the privilege of worshiping God in Christ, known in the fellowship of the Holy Spirit which is the one, holy, catholic, and apostolic church. The Spirit of God works with us in doing that job. He is the great missionary of Christ, and by his empowering and his inspiring, those who have shared the Spirit in the church are to be missionaries, too, wherever they may be. We can only worship God rightly if with true love and active effort and zeal we seek to share with other people the privilege of worship. The task is laid upon us so to witness and work that our worship will indeed be "in truth"; so to live as Christians that through us the Spirit may be seen active in the world. The work of the Spirit in worship leads directly to the work of the Spirit in our own lives; and the work of the Spirit in our own lives brings other men and women to see that the Spirit is indeed at work in our worship.

But is not all that has been said in this chapter far too "idealistic"? Have we not been talking about a dream world, or a "dream church"? I do not think so. And to show why I disagree I shall give two illustrations of worship from my own experience.

One has to do with a parish church in England; the other, a simple service I once attended in the chapel of an American college.

In the parish to which I refer the chief service is the Holy Communion, celebrated at 9:45 each Sunday with simplicity but with dignity. The church building is usually well filled, for the parish is in a large town which has a considerable number of active Christian laypeople. But there is another reason for the attendance. This parish is one in which there is a very keen sense of Christian responsibility in the world and in that town. Such English movements as Christian Aid, Shelter, the Simon Community, and the Samaritans, are not only welcomed but actively supported. Young people are provided with an opportunity for meetings where nobody frowns on their antics but everybody is glad that they are willing to use the church. The clergy are conscientious in welcoming strangers, even the "outcasts" of society, like homosexuals, drug addicts, and vagrants who know that they can come into the building when they are tired and be helped to get food when they are hungry. None of the clergy is a "pulpit orator" (thank God!), but all of them have learned how to preach Christ, the loving Father who sent him, and the acceptance by God in Christ of any and every man, woman, or child, just as he is, without questions asked or moral requirements set up for "admission." In every way, that parish is a center of civic life; yet it has also been outstanding in its boldness in supporting movements for social righteousness, racial understanding, and the recognition of goodwill in humanists and secularists.

Worship in that church is *real* worship because it is in touch with *real* life and hence in contact with the only *real* God—the God of this world's troubles and joy, its suffering and rejoicing. You can feel its reality as you take part in the eucharistic action, for you can sense that those present really *care*. The Spirit of God is inspiring and empowering the worshipers as they make their response to God in him who *is* the divine Response to the Father through Christ.

In the college chapel in the United States the situation is different, of course. At the service I attended, some twenty students and four faculty members gathered round a plain table in the crypt of the building. It was noonday. The table was spread with a linen cloth; on it were the vessels for Holy Communion. All of us sat, stood, or knelt at that table. The celebrant read the words of one of the new American liturgies, but there were times when he paused in the prayer of intercession and students spoke the names of a friend, a lover, somebody in trouble. We all received the sacrament, passing the bread around the table one to another; so also with the cup. When it was finished, the linen cloth was removed. Then we sat down together to a simple lunch of sandwiches, milk, or (believe it or not!) beer if we wished it—at that same table, mind you. We were a family in Christ; even the dullest visitor would have felt the reality of the fellowship. The "in-Spirited" community of young and old who having committed themselves to God in Christ were, in this worship and in the common meal which followed, cemented into an amazing unity.

I asked the chaplain what effect this small group had on the college. In no spirit of pride he told me that their influence was immeasurable. No longer did other undergraduates sneer at Christianity or talk condescendingly about "Christers," the collegiate Americanism for committed Christian people. They had been won to respect them, and some of them won to participation. That little group was the sponsor of *every* college movement for peace and for social, economic, and racial understanding. The chaplain told me of money raised, demonstrations attended, help given to lonely or dejected fellow students and even to some members of the staff. I was astounded. But should I have been? Certainly not, for here was a living witness to the abiding truth that when the church, even in such a tiny fragment as that college group, *is* the church, then the Spirit-filled Body of Christ is present and responsive to people.

Response is the peculiar "economy" of the Holy Spirit wherever he is at work. When Christian worship is truly "responsive" to God's act in Christ, it is the working of the Holy Spirit that makes it so. Our fitful and partial human responding is awakened by him, strengthened by him, and then taken by him into his own divine response as he conforms the creation to the loving purpose of God in the world's creative advance. So he is truly "at work in our worship."

103

8

The Spirit at Work in Our Lives

We are familiar with the fact that words in any language change their meaning from age to age. A good example is the word prevent, whose Latin original *prevenire* for hundreds of years governed the meaning of the English word derived from it: Prevent signified "going before," "coming in advance of expectation," "prior activity," etc. Today, as we all know, the word prevent suggests putting a stop to something or averting its happening. Hence a prayer found in the English *Book of Common Prayer* is generally misunderstood by ordinary people when they hear it read: "Prevent us, O Lord . . ." This suggests to many that we are asking God to stop us from doing something, whereas the original intention was to pray that God would always precede us, go before us, prepare for us the way in which to walk.

An even more considerable change in meaning has taken place with respect to the word comfort. Originally this word meant, as did its Latin original, strength, refreshment, or invigoration. The English word has the two Latin words *cum* (with) and *fortis* (strong) behind it. But that word comfort was later used for two very different ideas. It suggested "ease" or "giving another reassurance when that one is in trouble." Even this double-meaning is now being lost, however; when we use comfort as a noun we generally intend the meaning "ease." We have in our minds a picture of someone sitting comfortably in an armchair, before a fire, his feet on a hassock, a pipe in his mouth, an interesting book in his hand, and leisure time to enjoy himself. Hence the phrase "Comfortable Words" in the communion service gives the wrong impression to many who hear them. They are very far from suggesting their original sense, which was to strengthen, refresh, invigorate, make strong, and provide absolute reassurance.

The noun Comforter, in many English translations of the New Testament, in Prayer Book phrases, and in much well-known Christian literature, is applied to the Holy Spirit. When first used, it was intended to translate a Greek word which meant advocate or one who pleads on our behalf, and along with these included the idea of a fortifier or strengthener who refreshes and vitalizes people's lives with the strong current of his divine energy. This is the sense of the word in John's Gospel where the Holy Spirit is portrayed as acting in a vigorous fashion. The change in meaning of the English word, plus the unfortunate habit of Victorian hymn writers to dwell on the soft and sentimental (as in the familiar hymn, "Our blest Redeemer, ere he breathed . . ."), has almost entirely destroyed the dynamic and energizing picture of the Spirit for thousands of churchpeople—if they think of him at all.

This long excursus on the change in the meaning of a word will have served its purpose if it has suggested to the reader the need to look carefully at words used in ancient and familiar religious forms. Above all, it may have made clear that when we speak of the Holy Spirit we must eradicate any idea of comfort in the vulgar modern sense of the term and must think instead of the Holy Spirit as pressing through us, in us, and with us. This comfort, sometimes with gentle persuasion and occasionally with a shattering compulsion, is exercised on our weak and distorted human illusions, lies, and distortions, but always working with vigor and in the energizing power of active outgoing love.

In no area in which the Spirit works is it so important to see him in this active and dynamic mood as it is in the realm of personal human life. The Holy Spirit is at work in our lives. He is at work, not to make us comfortable in the modern meaning of that word, but to make us strong in our Christian discipleship, dedicated in our membership of the Christian fellowship, and bold in our witness for the truth which is in Christ Jesus. This chapter is to be devoted to a discussion of the working of the Spirit in people's lives. But as we shall see, that working is not confined to the Christian believer, but is in *all* people—although there is a special sense in which he may be said to act within the Christian.

Because the Holy Spirit is universal in his operation, as we argued in speaking of him "at work in the world," he is therefore at work in the lives of all of us and in the life of each of us. These are two sides of one truth: The Holy Spirit energizes through humanity, both individually and collectively. In his pervasive social action he brings people together in the service of great purposes, he molds the common life in such a way that the nations of the earth are brought into closer community one with the other, he moves to inspire and fortify the forces which strive for righteousness and justice everywhere in the world, he continually lures people to struggle for a "better world," he urges the people of all lands to conform the order of human society more closely to the will of God for their peaceful coexistence. And as he does all this, he shatters men's complacent self-interest so that they find themselves impelled to cooperate toward righteous ends.

We must here repeat that God the Holy Spirit works in such areas under an incognito. To recognize him *as* Holy Spirit is not so important as to serve instrumentally for the accomplishment of the goals which he sets. These goals are usually proposed to people in secular terms, like social and economic justice. They may seem to many to have no particularly religious quality in any obvious sense, but they do indeed. Yet as William Temple used to say, there is no reason to think that God is particularly interested in religion. For people some religious orientation is essential, since it is their way of establishing a relationship with God in an attentive and conscious manner. But God himself, who obviously does not have a religion, is much more concerned with the securing of the good ends which will both fulfill his creation's potentialities and also achieve his purpose in the creation.

The scientist seeks after truth. The artist tries to express his vision of harmony among contrasts which we call beauty, the statesman strives to secure justice among the nations, the soldier may selflessly give his life for his comrade-in-arms, the mother sacrifices herself for her children and their welfare. The carpenter works honestly at his workbench, the manual laborer digs a ditch not only to earn an honest day's wage but to contribute (albeit often without vivid awareness) to the public good. In these and in every other sphere of human life, there is an anonymous or incognito working of God, and hence a working of the Holy Spirit of God. As people seek to live as people, conforming their lives to whatever glimpse they may have had of truth, striving to do whatever good is possible for them to do, laboring to act righteously and to bring justice to others, God is at work; the Holy Spirit is moving through their lives to bring about their proper fulfillment as children of God.

It is tragically true that people are often very seriously misguided or mistaken in their grasp of what is right and good, beautiful and just. And almost inevitably, because of their human finite understanding, they fail to see the full reality of the goals after which they strive. Equally plain is the fact that people are prone perversely to deny or carelessly to ignore the plain facts; nobody but a blind fool could think that things are otherwise in this world. Yet even then, in that very imperfection and failure and distortion, the Holy Spirit is working—he is taking whatever good has been seen and done, correcting subtly whatever error or evil has been present, and making everything serve in the long run toward the accomplishment of the divine purpose in the creative advance which we call the world. It is a denial of Christian faith if we think to *remove* God the Holy Spirit from his world, and we sin in our thinking if we seek to *confine* the Holy Spirit to the specifically (we might also say narrowly) religious aspects of human life. Unless the Christian above all others recognizes this secular working of the Holy Spirit, he or she will be guilty of parochialism, provincialism, and an inverted religiosity in thought.

Christian people are now paying the penalty for their failure

107

to understand this. There are distinguished thinkers, themselves of Christian background, who have been so appalled by what I have just styled "inverted religiosity" that they have been prepared to give up the concept of God altogether and talk instead of a "religionless Christianity" whose chief concern is to implement righteousness and love in the world with no outreach beyond the merely human. They are sadly wrong in this; yet their position can be understood when we remember "how much evil has been done in the name of religion." That saying by the ancient Latin poet Lucretius is altogether too true for any believer in God to forget. Other people entirely devoted to God and to his revelation in Christ, like Dietrich Bonhoeffer, the German martyr to Nazism, have felt obliged to attack religiosity as one of the most dangerous enemies to genuine faith in God and honest service of God in the world. If we look carefully at what is behind such reactions, we see outraged protest at the confining of God and his Holy Spirit to the religious realm alone.

But we have said enough about this. We must now urge that while any thoughtful Christian must acknowledge both the wide cosmic working of the Spirit and his anonymous or incognito activity in human affairs everywhere, one must also (precisely because one *is* a thoughtful Christian) insist that in personal life, specifically personal religious life in its best sense, one has come to know most deeply the working of the Spirit. *Because* one has known the Spirit there, one has been able to recognize him at work elsewhere.

One place in which the Spirit is intimately known to people personally is their conscience. Here we need to be careful lest we suggest that any deliverance of the "inner voice" is necessarily and immediately the message of God's Spirit to us. Conscience is not an automatic device which will tell us God's will. Sometimes it is an uninformed conscience which only tells us what society has come to accept as conventional morality; sometimes it is but our own hidden desires emerging into our conscious minds. Conscience needs to be educated, enlightened, trained, developed; it must be accompanied by careful, clear, and honest thinking about the moral issues concerning which we are required to make decisions. It needs to be exposed to the best that has been thought on moral matters by Christians in the past and it needs to be aware of the many new facts which have been discovered in the present. At the same time, once we have taken the trouble to instruct our conscience, we can feel confident that here the Holy Spirit does speak to people, guiding them onward in their lives and intimating to them the kind of decisions which will be in accordance with God's will for them.

One of our difficulties is that thanks to a long tradition of negative morality, more concerned with telling us what *not* to do than to suggest to us positively what *to* do, many of our contemporaries have come to assume that conscience is what a French cynic once said: "a little voice that says 'No' so soon as we begin to enjoy ourselves." In reaction to such a negative conception of conscience, many others have rejected all thought of guidelines or hints about moral behavior and have come to believe that they should act as they happen to feel at any given moment. The result is antinomianism or moral lawlessness. I should be dishonest if I did not admit that of these two absurd alternatives I am inclined to feel more sympathetic with the latter than with the former! My reason for this preference is that it is altogether too apparent that the *negative* view of conscience, taken alone, tends to be a dangerous sanctifying of conventional respectability, and I agree with Robert Louis Stevenson that there is no more horrid "damper on the free spirit of man" than *this* sort of respectability. On the other hand, it is clear that one who does not think conscientiously about one's own moral decisions, in whatever area they may be required, is likely to be highly irresponsible; this irresponsibility can damage one's own life and can be equally harmful to those around the individual.

Our best approach to conscience is to see it as intimating ways in which we can "avoid the evil, and do the good," to use the phrase by which Thomas Aquinas defined natural moral law. Conscience will not then be infallible, since it is conditioned by finite human knowledge and limited human insight. But it will be trustworthy, provided only that in what we style our conscientious decisions we have remembered always to keep our eyes open and to use our heads. Then we can rightly speak of conscience as one of the ways in which God the Holy Spirit guides us toward truth and offers to us possibilities which will be for our best good and for the best good of others, thus indicative of God's will for us to follow.

One does not need to be particularly religious and certainly not specifically Christian to see that conscience is important. Therefore we should see that the place where the Holy Spirit most plainly acts, so far as Christian life is concerned, is not in the matter of conscience; rather, it is in the human response in loyalty, dedication, and service to Jesus Christ. The clearest trace of the Spirit's movement in personal life is in the desire of the disciple to be like his Lord, to serve that Lord to the best of his ability, and to reflect in his daily living the same quality of outgoing charity which marked the Lord when he was with us "in the flesh." That is to say, the Holy Spirit is best known to the Christian in the pressure of love in one's heart and in the compulsion to be helpful, brave, kindly, honest, open, and caring in all one's dealings with people. The Spirit works to make the disciple a person who is ready to give aid to the needy, to seek them out and provide for them; he works to make the disciple stand for the good and the right and to act accordingly.

In the impulse to sacrificial living there is another intimate working of the Holy Spirit. We have spoken earlier of *ascesis*, the athletic determination to strip oneself of unnecessary luggage so that the Christian "may run with patience the race that is set before" one: This is a movement of the Holy Spirit. Of course, self-discipline can be self-destructive when it is carried to absurd limits. There is no reason to think that the good things of the world are entirely to be abjured, as if they were not good but evil—here is the lamentable extreme to which the "Manichean" spirit can go. That spirit looks at the world and the things of the world and says that because those things are usually material, physical, and sensible (open to experience through the human sense), they cannot therefore be good for "spiritual beings." But the spirit which animates this sort of world-rejection is not the *Holy* Spirit; it is a perverse and lying spirit which the Jewish and Christian traditions have constantly been obliged to fight. This is the case even when we find some Christians falling victim to such a negative view of the world. True Christian asceticism never thinks the world evil. What it purposes is to use the things of and in the world so that the main drive of human

110

life is not thwarted but enabled to direct itself toward the supreme good which is God—and this can be through the things of the world when properly used and properly controlled.

This point is so important that it is worth dwelling on a little longer. The kind of piety which claims to be peculiarly and especially "spiritual" because it refuses to accept our human material condition is a constant threat to wholesome and soundly biblical Christian acceptance of the creation as the sphere of the divine activity—the divine milieu, as Teilhard de Chardin delighted to call it. That is to say, healthy Christian discipleship is positive. It is *world-accepting*, in that it takes the world as the sphere of God's working. It is also *world-transforming*, however, in that it wishes to make the world more adequately the sphere where God's will is in fact done. Hence the Christian does not reject or renounce life as one finds it; rather, the Christian seeks to use and enjoy it in the way best adapted to the effecting of goodness and love in one's own life and in those of others.

This suggests to us the way in which the Holy Spirit is known in Christian devotion or prayer. Far from being an escape from the world in which we live, Christian prayer is involvement in that world. When the neo-Platonist philosopher Plotinus spoke of "the flight of the alone to the Alone," he was talking of something that no instructed Christian ought ever to contemplate. No person is alone with God, despite the solitariness which establishes selfhood as one's own. Every person is with God in company with other people, summing up in one's own human existence the natural factors and the physical aspects of the creation. Thus the kind of mysticism which would think of union with God as an escape is utterly non-Christian—it is a denial of the incarnational and sacramental view of life upon which the Christian position is based. There is no reason for any person to try to be more spiritual than God himself; to attempt this is to blaspheme God and his creation. God willed to be in and with his creation. This is the only God whom we know—and this is the God who, among other world-directed activities, took it upon himself to be intimately united with his creation in the Man Christ Jesus. This is also the God who through material elements such as bread and wine, and by physical actions like washing with water, gives his grace and his strength to his children. And this is the God whose Spirit "filleth the world," which means the natural order and the outward activities of people, as well as the inner spiritual being of his children.

The Spirit who in the New Testament phrase prays with and in us is the same Spirit who is the responsive agent to God's declared purpose everywhere. Thus our praying, where we may sense the working of the Spirit in a most intensive degree, must be in accordance with this worldly condition in which all people live and where the Spirit operates. Here is no place to outline a theology of Christian prayer; we need only observe that prayer which is truly "in the Spirit" is prayer which moves toward making us more genuinely persons in society and the world, not disembodied spiritual creatures.

This brings us to the working of the Spirit which is directed toward the integration of human personality as it moves forward to fulfillment. Every human life needs some patterning if it is not to be reduced to chaos. But what is the right patterning of a human life? The Christian answer is that this has been revealed to people in the person of Jesus Christ. How then is a person to make that right patterning effectual in one's own existence? The Christian answer is that this is done through the action of the Holy Spirit within oneself. A life which is without ordering is a life which is scattered or chaotic, and hence (in the strictly proper meaning of the word) dissipated. That is the condition of many of us today. Our life lacks order, dignity, significance, and the beauty which is harmonious adjustment of the inevitable contrasts our experience produces. Because of this lack, many could say of themselves what in Acts Peter is reported to have said of the people of his generation: They were *skolios*, which is a Greek way of saying "going around in circles," without point and purpose.

Psychologists tell us that personal integration is a requirement for healthy human life. They have devised methods by which a patient can be led to understand oneself and one's motivations in such a fashion that one is enabled to accept one's own nature as it stands and then to strive to achieve the mode of existence proper to the self. They are entirely right in this approach and their contribution has been tremendous. But if they interpret integration in terms of the mere adjustment of people to the social conventions of the group to which they belong, they may very well do more harm than good to troubled persons. Happily the more discerning of them see much more deeply into the situation. Experts such as Erich Fromm have grasped the fact that the only true integration making possible the proper fulfillment of human potentiality is in the urgent desire to love—to give oneself in love and to be open to receive from others the love which they may be prepared to offer. Although not all the experts would use the words which Dr. Fromm eagerly uses, they acknowledge (perhaps quite unconsciously) that the basic adjustment of people is to God who *is* Love. In relationship to love-in-action, human life can find dignity and meaning, beauty and ordering. This is genuinely normal human existence— normal meaning here the pattern which is proper to people and which empirically we so often lack.

If these psychologists see the point, a Christian surely ought to see it too, and then also see behind it the power of the Holy Spirit. It is a power that is molding and shaping our disorganized and disordered living, luring us on toward the pattern of perfection which is the true person—or Luther rightly said "the *proper* man"—Jesus Christ. The man or woman who is gradually being conformed to that pattern is on the way to a *normal* life. Such a life is a gathering together of every aspect of human nature—its desires, drives, and impulses; its physical equipment and functioning; its aspirations and hopes; its love and yearning for union with others; and its seeking after an enduring reality with whom it may be in fellowship in such a manner that the whole person is included. This is integration in its highest sense. When we see someone who is like that, we call such a one a "saint."

Sainthood, however, does not mean removal from the world. Nor does it suggest a sort of steam-roller removal of all the distinctive qualities of the particular person, for no genuine sanctity is destructive of the talents, tastes, and capacities of the man or woman whom we respect and admire. The saints are very different one from another. Between Francis of Assisi and John Wesley, Theresa of Avila and Theresa of Lisieux, George Herbert and Martin Luther King, there is a difference of personal quality that often astounds us. But there is *one* thing that makes

113

all these men and women truly saints in the Christian meaning of that term. All of them were open to the Spirit of God as he conformed them to the pattern of personhood in Jesus Christ. We have no reason to fear that such conformation will make us less human than we were before. On the contrary, it will make us more fully human, when all of us are caught up into and made more like the Man whom as Christians we desire to follow, imitate, and serve.

In the last chapter we spoke about the way in which the Holy Spirit is at work in Christian worship. One part of that worship is the singing of hymns about the Spirit. Another is the saying of prayers which often, like the hymns, include a reference to the Holy Spirit, asking that he may assist us in our worship as in our lives. Frequently the language of those prayers and hymns is difficult for modern minds. But that may well be because we persistently refuse to employ in religious thinking the imagination which we allow elsewhere. It may also be because we are too intent on specifically identifying the Spirit as present and thus insufficiently prepared to see him *in what he does*.

A familiar hymn, often sung by Christians at ordinations or during Whitsuntide, runs as follows:

> Come, thou Holy Spirit, come!
> And from thy celestial home
> Shed a ray of light divine!
> Come, thou Father of the poor!
> Come, thou source of all our store!
> Come, within our bosoms shine!
>
> Thou, of comforters the best;
> Thou, the soul's most welcome guest;
> Sweet refreshment here below;
> In our labor, rest most sweet;
> Grateful coolness in the heat;
> Solace in the midst of woe.
>
> O most blessed Light divine,
> Shine within these hearts of thine,

And our inmost being fill!
Where thou art not, man hath naught,
Nothing good in deed or thought,
Nothing free from taint of ill.

Heal our wounds, our strength renew;
On our dryness pour thy dew;
Wash the stains of guilt away;
Bend the stubborn heart and will;
Melt the frozen, warm the chill;
Guide the steps that go astray.

On the faithful, who adore
And confess thee, evermore
In thy sev'n-fold gift descend;
Give them virtue's sure reward;
Give them thy salvation, Lord;
Give them joys that never end.

I have quoted this hymn in full because it may present a great
many difficulties to modern people. Much of the imagery seems
strange to us if we think too literally about it. Some of the ideas
may no longer have much meaning for us today. But two things
need to be said about the hymn.

First, its imagery is meant to be taken with imagination. No
poetry should be taken in the strictly literal sense of the words.
We would be foolish if we interpreted Robert Burns's familiar
line "my luv is like a red red rose" as requiring a botanical
analysis of the young lady to whom he was referring. Hence we
need to remember what Dr. Richard Kroner has called "the
religious function of the imagination." If there is any place in
which imaginative thought is necessary, it is in religious life and
worship.

Second and much more important is the possibility of turning
the familiar phrases round in order to grasp their significance.
In the hymn the Spirit is invoked to give coolness, balm, refreshment, strength, forgiveness, light, warmth of heart, devotion to
Christ, and rest. But suppose we say that from time to time we
have such a sense of coolness in the heat of conflict; such balm

or healing in the wounds that life inflicts on us; such refreshment when we are weary of struggle; such strength when we feel weak; such forgiveness when we know ourselves to have offended our brothers or to have violated God's will of love; such light when everything appears dark to us; such warmth of heart when our whole life seems chilled and our desire to love has been frozen within us; such devotion to Christ when we recognize the inadequacy of our commitment; and such rest when we are exhausted in soul and body. Suppose we say that when this happens to us and in us, what is *really* happening is that the Holy Spirit is at work in our personal lives. Then we shall be able to see what the hymnwriter was really driving at: coolness, rest, courage in adversity, commitment to Christ, and all the rest are nothing other than the grace of God given through the Spirit to people on their pilgrimage in this world. We do not always recognize that what happened is indeed a working of God the Spirit. But the Christian is one who should recognize that it is the Spirit of God who has done, is doing, and will do these things.

Many years ago a saintly parson of my acquaintance was asked a very simple question by a child. The child asked, "Where does the sky begin?" The clergyman at once responded, "The sky begins in your lungs." I like that story; I think it is worth thinking about. It is indeed true that the sky, by which one supposes the child meant the air which was all about him, stretching up to the remote stars, begins in our lungs as we breathe. Where, then, does the work of God the Holy Spirit begin, so far as our personal knowledge of him goes? The answer is that the work begins in our human lives where we are brought to respond to whatever we have been given to know of God and about God. Supremely that work begins for the Christian man or woman when he or she responds to Jesus Christ in his Body the church. It begins as such a person lives by the sacraments, prays, reads the scriptures, is prepared to offer oneself for use by God as God is known in the Christian fellowship's age-long tradition, and seeks to love others in the church and others outside the church, in sincerity and truth.

When we put ourselves in that position of faithful acceptance of God the Holy Spirit moving through the community of faith, we will begin to know that God has given his Spirit to his human children in a very special mode through the fellowship of Christian commitment. Then perhaps we shall come to rejoice in that Spirit and be ready to say without question that the Holy Spirit is at work in the world, in worship, in prayer, and in human life. Maybe too we will be able to make our own the words of the psalmist who said that he was glad "in the operations of his hands"—the hands of the divine Spirit who "filleth all things," who unites believers in the Christian life of discipleship, who ceaselessly labors in secular as well as religious realms, and whose unique "economy" is to awaken and empower a response through the whole creation to God's perfect love as this is declared in Jesus Christ.

9

The Holy Spirit
in God

Some readers may think that a great deal of what has been said in this book is simply assertion. In a way one would be correct in thinking so. But the truth is that the assertion has been nothing other than the assertion of Christian faith both in its implications and applications. Further, it springs from the life of the Christian in the fellowship of the church, interpreted and given context in Christian theology. Now we must turn to that theological context and conclude our study with a discussion of the meaning and place of the Holy Spirit in the Godhead—in other words, we must deal with what in classical theology is called the doctrine of the Holy and Undivided Trinity.

What sense, however, can such a doctrine have for us today? Certain theologians say, "It makes no sense. The only thing to do is retain the old language as a useful symbol which unites us with the past ages of Christian faith, while we acknowledge that trinitarian talk is no longer tenable theologically speaking." I believe that such theologians are making a very grave mistake, and this chapter is an attempt to show why. On the other hand, all of us must admit that a good deal of the detail and precision with which trinitarian theology has been worked out in the past is more an evidence of human presumption than a necessary consequence of the data given in Christian faith as it is lived in the church. Yet the overweening pride of intellect which has led to such extraordinary claims to knowledge of the innermost secrets of the divine existence ought not to prevent us from trying to make what sense we can of the divine reality in terms of its self-revelation to people.

It is my contention that triunitarian thought—I prefer the word triunitarian since it is less suggestive of a tritheistic view than the more common word trinitarian—provides an insight into that divine reality which we shall disregard or deny at our own peril. Why is this? Largely because the point of triunitarianism is not so much in its logical meaning as in its capacity to focus and give significance to Christian worship and life. Indeed the *Quicumque Vult* or Athanasian Creed says as much: "This is the Catholic faith: that we *worship* one God in Trinity and Trinity in Unity." That statement is clear enough; and its application is in the whole range of theological discourse, which is not speculative or theoretical talk but the provision of context for adoration and discipleship.

Let us recall what was said in the second chapter about the dynamic view of the world. The world is a process which is being made; it is not a finished product. In the process, there is genuine continuity but at the same time there is the appearance of equally genuine novelty. The movement is toward the realization of potentiality, each entity or occasion having been provided with an initial aim which, through decision among relevant possibilities, it may bring to actuality. The goal toward which each entity moves is its "subjective aim"; but the achievement of that aim is not automatic. It requires the use of the available material, with the choice of possibilities for good and the elimination or rejection of other possibilities which will not promote good. It is always possible that the wrong choices may be made. When they are made the ongoing movement can be twisted or there can be lags or backwaters, so that fulfillment is denied or adequate and proper fulfillment is prevented.

At levels below conscious choice, there is an element of decision in that certain possibilities are accepted and others rejected. But at the level of conscious choice, such as we know in those societies of entities we call human life, there is *responsibility* for right or wrong choosing. That is where we stand in the ongoing process. We can either take or not take the steps which will lead to the making of personality. But no person lives alone, nor does any other entity in the process stand in isolation from the rest. All are related in a rich and complex interpenetration, so that what is decided *here* will affect what is decided there also. There is a give-and-take which is the very nature of process as a social movement, not as a discrete and insulated series.

In this ongoing of creation as process, the dominant factor is the purpose of God whose nature is love-in-action. He is intimately related with every part of the process as a whole and also with each occasion as it comes into existence, as it moves toward fulfillment (or lack of fulfillment), and as it makes (or fails to make) its proper contribution to the total social good. But God is not a remote metaphysical principle, invoked as a satisfactory logical explanation of the existence of everything else. He is to be interpreted in terms of the world in which he is working. While in some respects he is entirely unique, for example in being a persistent entity or series of entities who cannot perish, he is also the chief exemplification of whatever principles are required to make sense of the world. He is transcendent, both because he is distinctively himself and also because he is utterly inexhaustible in resources, indefatigable in his working, and in the long run able to bring the creation to its proper fulfillment—not by overriding the free decision of the creaturely events, however, but rather by his molding and shaping of them, and by his acceptance of their achievements for good which become an opportunity for further advance. He works in the lower levels of creation by exerting some measure of coercion to keep them from getting entirely out of harmony with the driving purpose of good which is their raison d'etre, but this coercive action is minimal. His *actual* nature as God and his chief manner of operation in creation is through persuasion or love. He draws the world to himself by his loving care; he shares in its sorrows as well as in its joys; he "incarnates" himself in every bit of it, as he unceasingly and faithfully works to secure for everything its proper good.

At the creaturely human level of conscious awareness and

attention, he makes himself available to those creatures for a more personal relationship with them; hence he is known in certain kinds of experience, including moral and aesthetic apprehension and the kind of sharing which is like personal human relations. He is indeed essentially love—"pure unbounded love" —and hence he discloses himself in the created order as just that. Especially in highly significant moments, which are important because they provide decisive evidence of the nature of the ongoing drive to fulfillment, he is disclosed for what he is. Christians claim, on the basis of all that his life has effected in this world, that Jesus Christ is the supreme focal point of this divine self-disclosure. In their response to that historical event which they call by Christ's name, they find themselves empowered and strengthened to go forward toward the fulfillment of their possibilities as people—they become persons "in Christ," who is accepted by them as both the pattern of human life in its excellence and as the expression in human terms of the activity of God as love. In being and doing these things, Christ is no denial of whatever else is good or true in human experience or in the created order. On the contrary, he is both the coronation and the correction of all other goodness or truth. The uniqueness which is claimed for him is not absolute, as if he were unrelated to all else, but is inclusive of all prior, concomitant, or subsequent disclosures of the basic nature of the whole cosmic enterprise. And the same universal significance is found in the response made to Christ *and to all good.*

Now the argument which this chapter proposes is that in this setting, provided for our thinking by modern science and enquiry and by a profound understanding of what life teaches us from our own experience as well as from observation—in this setting, the insight of the Christian ages regarding the triune nature of Godhead makes sense. It is an intimation or glimpse of the truth about God, even if the detailed working out of the doctrine in earlier ages presents problems because it sometimes appears to claim knowledge that no finite man could ever honestly and humbly profess to have about the mystery of the divine life. Despite those difficulties, however, there is deep wisdom in the triunitarian formulation, and it would be folly to throw it away as so much "old stuff" which is of no use to us today and which had better be discarded from our thinking about this most important of all matters: Who is God, what is he like, and how best can we conceive him and his action?

The first thing to be said is that the triune conception of God, whatever else it may have to offer, provides a symbolic picture of the interdependence of personality and sociality. We have noted the inescapable fact that the more adequately a person attains fulfillment of one's own possibilities, the more open one is both in receiving from and in giving to others. Despite a very prevalent misunderstanding, individual and person are not simply different words for the same thing. An individual is one of a given species or type, but not necessarily in intimate relationship with others of that same species or type. A person is of necessity a participant in the lives of others of the race. In a universe in which this person-in-relationship pattern is found at the human level, analogies to it are discovered elsewhere—the whole world is organic or societal, each event in it affecting all and all having influence on each. This truth is patent to the observer who knows himself participant in the created order; God himself is not an exception to it. The doctrine of the triunity of God is a way of saying that in him there is the perfect realization of the person-society relationship.

That is the first main point which I wish to stress. But from it there follows another. If this is true in respect to the actuality of God himself, it is also true in respect to God's relationships with the creation. There are indeed diversities in his manner of relationship with the world. First of all, he is active in the world as the agency which supplies the initial aim for each entity. In this respect he is creative of genuine novelty, for each entity is a new unity and not simply a repetition of others. Each entity has its own proper aim to fulfill, as if it were given a vocation to which to respond. Thus the old doctrine that God creates ex nihilo—out of nothing save himself—is true enough, but in a rather different sense from the conventionally given one. There is the continual ongoing of the creative process, to be sure. Creativity or the potentiality to achieve actuality is always present, coeternal with the divine yet not independent of it. But the particular aim which each entity is to realize out of that creative potentiality is given to it through the divine decision to see

122

actualized this rather than that particular "item" in the vast, even infinite, continuum of possibility. *Here God is seen as the ultimate determining source or cause.*

Second, there is the continuing thrust or drive for the fulfilling of this given possibility. An entity not only has its initial aim, achievement of which will give it final satisfaction. The entity also has a path to follow if that initial aim is indeed to become the subjective aim, through which the entity discovers its genuine, intentional, and fulfilling satisfaction. Here too God is at work. He ordains the expression which will be in accordance with his will. This expression is the intentional perfection of each entity and each society of entities. The expression is enacted at appropriate levels. And in human life such an expression is enacted in the manhood of Jesus Christ. His manhood, with its conditioning and environing factors (what prepared for it, what surrounded it, what results it accomplished), is for Christian faith the visible human expression of the divine intention. It is the self-expression of the divine purpose for the human race. But it is also more than that, since it is the self-expression of the divine himself. The purpose of God for people is that they "become and remain human," become fully what they are potentially. In becoming such, there is necessarily also the disclosure of the divine in terms which people can understand, grasp, and receive. *Here God is seen as self-expressive, but always in ways which are available for and open to reception by the particular level of creative process which is in view.*

Thirdly, as the argument in this book intends to show, there is a necessary receptivity and responsiveness in the creative advance. Each entity, having received its initial aim and having known however dimly the way in which fulfillment of that aim is both an expression of its own identity and a manifestation of the divine purpose for it, is enabled in greater or less degree to say its "Yes," to give its consent, to the realization of that aim or goal which will fulfill and satisfy it. In one sense, this is through the free decision made by each entity for itself, with all the circumambient factors that contribute to it and help to mold or shape it. But in a deeper sense, the possibility of such response or consent, as well as the degree to which the response or consent is given, depends upon all the factors throughout the universe which are relevant and effective in their bearing upon the entity. *Here God is working to bring about just such response or consent.*

We see a remarkable interrelationship of three differing modes of divine activity in and upon the creative process. God *creates* by providing initial aim; God lures by providing the *enacted pattern of self-expression;* God urges, and in his urging works for the *response* which will enable his creatures to become what that self-expression implies. There is a threefold activity. Yet the divine reality himself is the one God who is Love-in-action everywhere and always. If we put this in strictly theological terms, we may speak of God as *the creative source* of all novelty as well as the ordering power which prevents creation from disintegrating into chaos; of God as *self-expressive of his purpose*, which is nothing other than the achievement by the creation of its intended goal; and of God as *the moving power of response* which enables the creation to become in fact that which in intention it is meant to become. Thus God is Creative Source, Self-Expressive Act, and Responsive Movement. And he is *one God*. This is triunitarianism.

But God is always Love—at least in the Christian interpretation, he can be seen as this and only as this. Once again, the threefold pattern still holds. For Love is inexhaustible in its creativity; it is characterized by loving self-expression for those with whom it is in loving relationship; and it provides the motive-power for the realization of love—a motive power which itself is nothing other than love. A human analogy helps us here. It is essentially the analogy which Augustine must have had in mind when he used the triad "Lover-Beloved-Love" in the *De Trinitate* and which led him to stress so emphatically in the *Confessions* that only one who had genuinely loved could understand what he meant when he spoke of God in his love for the world. The human analogy would follow these lines. A person who is thoroughly and utterly loving, urgent in the desire to give of self, is able to provide for others the opportunities through which genuine love will be awakened in them and expressed by them. By the very fact of loving, one also makes it possible for them to respond to one's own outgoing toward them;

they are enabled to love in return, finding in that returning love their own joy and their own deep satisfaction.

The argument just given is perfectly valid so far as process thinking is concerned. It is also valid, I believe, in providing a way in which the triunitarian picture of God may be interpreted as the guarantee of two matters that are of the greatest importance. One of these is the social-personal quality which prevails throughout the cosmos and of which we have already spoken. The other is a conception of God which can claim for him the chief role in the ongoing of the process itself.

It will be noted that in the phrase "chief role in the ongoing of the process," the adjective chief should now be stressed. Whatever else a Christian may say about God, one should not say that he is the *only* agent in the creative process or advance. To say that would be to turn God into a tyrant, a dictator, a kind of super-Caesar who without allowing any freedom to his subjects simply forces them to do his will. Such a picture of God is thoroughly unchristian, no matter how many distinguished Christian thinkers have used it. As a matter of fact, even those thinkers have generally been careful to quality their talk about God's "almightiness" by adjectives or adverbs that guarantee some measure, however slight, of freedom and hence of responsibility to the creatures. Our approach to the subject was different, however. We did not begin with a concept that so emphasizes divine power and omnipotence that it requires subsequent radical modification in the light of ordinary human awareness of freedom and responsibility. Instead, we began with the concept of God as cosmic Love-in-action and we insisted that whatever power is attributed to God must *always* be interpreted in the light of that Love which he is. This entails a very considerable alteration in the meaning of the word power. It can no longer be seen as absolutely omnicompetent and overwhelming in its impact, but must now be taken as power-for-love, power-in-love, and power-by-love—and that is a very different matter.

Love-in-action can *never* be the only cause, for if it were its objects would not be treated as objects of love at all. We should be back in this "coercive power" position. Love demands that there shall be freedom and responsibility on the part of the loved object; only through such freedom and responsibility can love

125

effect anything whatever. God, then, is the *chief* agent in the creative process, providing initial aim out of his infinite resources, expressing himself in such a way that his creatures find in him the goal toward which they would strive, and working in them persuasively to secure the response which will both enrich the divine life and fulfill the creatures. Here is three-in-oneness; here is a triunity of operation which is a reflection in the created world of the social-personal reality of God himself.

When we talk in this way, we recognize that in certain respects we have departed from a good deal of the terminology as well as from much of the traditional way of envisaging the relationship of God to the world. We are not simply repeating the formal theological definition of deity as triunitarian. But it may be that such terminology was far too precise and that the conventional formulation of God's mystery and his relationship in the world was too dependent on absolutist ideas. Yet we may also think that the intention of the triunitarian theologians has been preserved, even if their definition is not so much discarded as given a new turn and a different importance.

So far our discussion may have seemed arid and abstract—of necessity, indeed, since the subject is not capable of concrete illustration save for our crucial and Christian example of what it means, humanly speaking, to love and to manifest love. In conclusion, let us now try to see how the triunitarian concept of God works out practically in respect to Christian worship, remembering the statement in the ancient creed *Quincumque Vult* that the faith is that "we worship one God in Trinity, and Trinity in Unity."

First, the faith is that we worship. If this suggested only what we do when we go to church to engage in an act of public worship, it would be misleading. Not that such public worship is unimportant, nor that our engaging in it is irrelevant—one whole chapter has attempted to show exactly the contrary. Yet by worship the *Quincumque* means something more profound than that. Worship here is intended to include the whole relationship of people to God. Worship is the governing attitude and principle of a person's life. In that case, the faith which we hold manifests itself in the way in which we live. It has to do with our whole posture or stance as Christians.

126

Then, second, to worship God as triune, as "Trinity in Unity," is to see and accept the threefold activity of God in his world. It is to recognize that it is from God that the initial aim or vocation which is ours comes to us. He is its source, not we ourselves. Recognizing this, we also perceive that the vocation which is given us is brought to fulfillment only when we are conformed to the self-expression of God for people in the perfect humanity set before us in Jesus Christ. He is the proper, the true, person; and he is this because he is the manifest disclosure of God himself to humanity. To worship God in this high sense is to let ourselves be open to the pressure of love within us, urging us to respond to that loving personhood in which God is self-expressed "for us men and for our salvation." God is thus worshiped in his "threeness," yet he is worshiped also in the unity which means that all this is *of* God and *is* God. At this point, we may recall Augustine's declaration that the "work of the 'persons' of the Trinity is undivided," is all of a piece, is indeed *one*. This is a way of insisting that God is the God of order, not of confusion. He is such because he is one God, the one supremely worshipful perfection and goodness.

Third, the ancient theological teaching about circumincession or *perichoresis* in Godhead has something valuable to tell us. This teaching said that the hypostases in the Godhead are coinherent, each abiding in the others, all of them sharing in the one common life which is compresent to all and which is subsistent in that sharing. The three work together because they are the one Godhead, yet with the distinctions which preserve both the richness and the diversity that in God are harmonized. So it is that to say that the Holy Spirit "proceeds from the Father through [not *and*] the Son" is to say that the creative source of every initial aim in the creation is known to us and operates on our behalf in terms of the Self-Expression which is the Word—Love enacted in the world supremely in Jesus Christ. At the same time it is to say that the Response which is made throughout creation, and in people, to that creative source as it is thus self-expressed is a genuine response not to some abstract, vague, or inchoate idea of love but precisely to the Love which is God and which is manifested in action in Jesus Christ.

I hope that in these last pages I have shown how the triunitarian conception of God, with all its difficulties, is a means by which basic Christian experience and important Christian insight may be nourished. Furthermore, I hope that I have done something to show that such experience and insight require a theological foundation. However this may be, the truth remains that whether we are trained theologians or simple believers, Christian faith in act, empowered through worship, may be summed up in words that are familiar to us from frequent repetition in liturgical prayer:

Let us bless the Father and the Son with the Holy Spirit:
Let us praise and exalt *him* forever.